HOLOCAUST WALL HANGINGS

by

Judith Weinshall Liberman

with essays by
Stephen C. Feinstein
Salvatore Scalora
Ori Z. Soltes
and by the artist

Photography by David Caras

JUDITH WEINSHALL LIBERMAN

Liberman@tiac.net

Printed in the United States of America
by
CHARLES RIVER LITHOGRAPHY
Rockland, Massachusetts

Distributed by
SCHOEN BOOKS
Seven Sugarloaf Street
South Deerfield
MA 01373 USA
413-665-0066
schoen@schoenbooks.com
www.schoenbooks.com

Library of Congress Control Number: 2002091156

ISBN 0-9719027-0-4

Contents

Introduction

In 1988, I began creating the Holocaust Wall Hangings. By then I had already completed a series of more than two dozen paintings about the Holocaust. The paintings had been done in acrylics and incorporated brush painting, block printing and stenciling. I felt that the medium I had used—paint on stretched canvas—could not fully convey my feelings about the Holocaust.

By using fabric as a background—and the Holocaust Wall Hangings are works on fabric—I could extend the size of the works and harness a wide variety of means to express myself. I could paint on the fabric and do block printing and stenciling, as I had done in the paintings; but I was able to introduce sewing, appliqué, embroidery and beading as well. The resulting surfaces and textures, added to those of the background fabric itself, broadened my means of expression far beyond what was possible in the paintings. The loose-hanging fabric promised to be significant in itself by evoking an image of banners of the Third Reich, which flew over Europe during the Holocaust.

In the Holocaust Wall Hangings, as in most of my work, color is used expressively rather than descriptively. To convey my feelings about the Holocaust, I found it necessary to employ, for the most part, a limited palette of red, gray and black. The choice seemed inevitable—red: blood and fire; gray: suffering and despair; black: death.

Like my Holocaust Paintings, the Holocaust Wall Hangings abound with repeated images: A body, a dismembered arm, a boxcar reappears in the same work. The repeated images are usually done by means of block printing. For some works, dozens of blocks are carved with similar (though not identical) images. The repetition of images is designed to underscore the relentlessness of the Holocaust.

The Holocaust Wall Hangings fall mainly into two distinct groups: First, there are the *Scenes of the Holocaust*. These works refer more or less to the visible world; in the continuum between realistic and abstract, they are closer to the former than to the latter. In most of the *Scenes*, people take center stage. They are seen as either utterly isolated or as part of a totally depersonalized mass. In either situation, the individual is portrayed as stripped of his/her humanity by the Holocaust.

In the second group, the *Maps of the Holocaust*, the Holocaust is depicted in more abstract terms.* Places and numbers, as well as other symbols of destruction, here take the place of the individual in telling the story. Often in these works, as in the *Scenes*, people appear, but this is done within the broader context of place and time.

The Holocaust Paintings had already consisted of

---

* I found information useful for creating the maps in Martin Gilbert's *Atlas of the Holocaust*.

Scenes on the one hand and *Maps* on the other. Although there were new *Scenes* and *Maps* to construct, my main task in creating the Holocaust Wall Hangings was, as I saw it, to maximize the power of my new medium in conveying my vision of the Holocaust.

After spending a decade creating artwork—both paintings and wall hangings—about the Holocaust, I began exploring my personal relationship with the subject of the Shoah. This I did in a series of mixed media works (combining collage and painting), the Self-Portraits of a Holocaust Artist, in which I placed myself in Holocaust settings as an act of empathy with the victims. Some of these works were later translated into Holocaust Wall Hangings. I called the sub-series *Epilogue*. Also included in this sub-series are wall hangings raising an artist's post-Holocaust questions about God. The *Epilogue* wall hangings thus express in a more direct way than the *Scenes* and *Maps* my personal feelings and thoughts about the Holocaust.

A question I am frequently asked by those who hear that my artwork focuses on the Holocaust is "Why?" If I shrug my shoulders in response, or answer that I am not sure what it is that drives me to it, persistent questions usually follow: Was I in the Holocaust? Were my parents? And how about the rest of my family? The fact is that neither I nor my parents nor anyone else in my immediate family was physically in the Holocaust. True to their Zionist ideal, my family—my parents, uncles, aunts, grandparents, even my great grandmother—came to Israel (then Palestine) circa 1921, long before Hitler, and stayed there for the rest of their lives. Naturally, I myself was born in Israel, and even though I was alive during the Holocaust, it was in Israel that I grew up and spent the war years, not in Europe.

Of course I was aware—as aware as a child could be— of what was going on in Europe. I was ten years old when World War II broke out, and still remember the announcement over the radio of Hitler's invasion of Poland and the somber expression on my father's face when he heard the news. For the following six years, I increasingly heard bits of information about the plight of the Jews of Europe, the ghettos, the camps, the killings. Some of those close to me lost loved ones at the hands of the Nazis. The grim news was everywhere; it was in the air we breathed and it became part of us.

It is reasonable to assume that but for the indelible impression that the war years made upon me, I would not be focusing my work on the Holocaust today. But there are probably other factors as well. One need not be a psychologist to realize that an artist's work has deep psychological roots; the choice of subject matter is rarely a conscious one for an artist. In the final analysis, however, it is not what drives me to create the Holocaust Wall Hangings that is important. What is important is that my Holocaust art, standing on its own independently of its creator, will speak to people's hearts. What is important is that tomorrow, one year from now, ten years from now, a hundred years from now someone somewhere contemplating the Holocaust Wall Hangings will be moved enough to look into his/her own heart and resolve to be human.

Acknowledgments

It is to the three people who were vitally important in shaping my life that I wish to express my indebtedness: to my husband, Prof. Robert Liberman, who died in 1986; to my father, Dr. Abraham Weinshall, who passed away in 1968; and to my brother, Saul Weinshall, whom I lost in 1948. Although each of these men contributed to my life in his own way, I firmly believe that all three played a crucial role in my eventual creation of the Holocaust Wall Hangings.

The Holocaust Wall Hangings are dedicated to the memory of my husband, Robert Liberman. As a young Air Force lieutenant, Robert was part of the United States forces that helped liberate Europe from the Nazis. The memory of what he saw in 1945, especially the camps, haunted him for the rest of his life. But it is not only because of his connection with the war that I have dedicated my work to Robert's memory. It is also—and mainly—because for the thirty-three years we were together he supported me, encouraged me, loved me beyond what I dreamed possible. It was his loyalty and devotion that gave me the strength to pursue art. If I learned to fly, it was because Robert was always there to catch me if and when I faltered.

My father, Dr. Abraham Weinshall, always was—and will forever remain—my standard for what is human. His wisdom and kindness, his honesty, his modesty, his loyalty and his dedication to the principles and causes he believed in have been my guiding light throughout my life. And although I know I can never measure up to him, the example he set inspires me to try.

My brother, Saul Weinshall, was killed in the Israeli War of Independence at the age of twenty-one. The memory of Saul's warmth and friendship, his enthusiasm and curiosity, is always with me. Often as I work on one of my Holocaust Wall Hangings I recall how, during the dark years of World War II, Saul refused to go down to the air-raid shelter of our home in Haifa but insisted, rather, on going out on the balcony to watch enemy bombers as they flew overhead. More than once we found shrapnel nearby after the air attack. Yet Saul was undeterred. His courage amazed me. It was shrapnel that caused Saul's mortal wound on the Egyptian front in 1948. In my work, I have always striven to make up, in some small measure, for Saul's untimely death.

Judith Weinshall Liberman

Conceptualizing the Scale of Destruction

Judith Weinshall Liberman's Wall Hangings about the Holocaust

by

Stephen C. Feinstein

"I was there for about two years. Time there is not the same as it is on earth. Each moment there moves at its own speed. The inhabitants of this planet had no names. They did not dress as we dress here. They were not born there, nor did they give birth. They breathed by other laws of nature. I believe with all my heart that as in astrology, the stars influence our fate. So the ash-planet Auschwitz stands over this earth and influences it. They went away from me, they kept going from me, always leaving me, and in our parting look—our vow—I can see them stare at me."

Holocaust Survivor Ka-Tsenik
from "The 81st Blow," film from Lochemai Hagetaot

The Holocaust as a subject for representation in the arts has intensified during the past ten years. More and more, artists, writers, poets, photographers and filmmakers are trying to grapple with the problems of conceptualizing this enormous event, hoping that art might be able to do what the study of history cannot—comprehend the annihilation of six million Jews and half a million Roma and Sinti (Gypsies) through the domination by a country that had, until 1933, been associated highly with the development of civilization and culture.

Unfortunately, the results have been mixed. Artistic representation, especially by people who were not "there," is complicated by many survivor-artists who state openly, such as Polish artist Jozef Szajna, that "those who were not there cannot paint about it," to Theodore Adorno, who had written at first that "after Auschwitz, there can be no lyric poetry." Adorno, however, eventually retracted this statement and admitted that it might be possible to have artistic representation of the Holocaust, just as a man being tortured has the right to scream.

Whatever one might think about philosophical debates on the subject, such issues are important for several reasons. First, there is the question of the authenticity of image. Certainly, painters who have tried to imagine the passion of Christ at Calvary have had to deal with this problem. How horrible was that event? And if it was too horrible, might representation of it drive the believers out of the church? Can those who were not in Auschwitz understand it and represent it? If art about this subject cannot be a reproduction true to actual images of persecution and death, will a metaphor suffice?

Secondly, the Holocaust was a public event, witnessed from its inception by bystanders, individuals and countries. It was covered in newspapers and was extensively photographed, not only from the ground, but also from the air. For many, the power of photography is so strong that painting and other representations seem pale.

Thirdly, despite all caveats, visual representation in the form of painting, sculpture, and in the case of Judith Liberman wall hangings, can provide a series of multiple ideas which serve as points of departure for understanding one or many aspects of the event better. To be sure, artists indulging in such work have to always be wary of misrepresentation. A painting need not be a narrative, but whatever its form, it must be true to the facts of the subject matter. Unlike other subjects of historical study, Holocaust denial exists and is a big business. Artists who stretch metaphors so wide as to make them formless do a disservice to the study of the Shoah. So, the line of acceptability has narrowing parameters.

Judith Liberman's Holocaust Wall Hangings, of which I first became aware from their installation at Yad Vashem in 1992, and then viewed them in the flesh at Liberman's exhibition at the DeCordova Museum in 1994, fall into a unique category. Obviously, they are constructed from narratives and memory of the event itself. Most uniquely, what strikes the viewer from the first, is the medium of fabric and sewn material, plus the monumental scale of each work.

Liberman has suggested that her use of fabric was to establish a dialectic between our usual associations with fabric—"the home, with permanence, with stability"—and the opposite reality of the German destruction of the Jews. But if collage is a specific artistic form of the twentieth century, the viewer in the case of Liberman's art is impelled to consider her artistic achievements as fabric collages, sometimes very structured with strong narratives. Others, however, are more abstract, which seem to ask the viewer to consider how the subject intrudes on various aspects of his or her own memory. One might also inquire if fabric and sewing are a particularly women's craft? Perhaps recently it has become so. However, there is a long history of tapestries from the Middle Ages that have become artistic treasures, not only because of their high quality as cloth-based items, but also because of their biblical narratives. Walking through museums even today, the viewer is often overwhelmed by the size of such tapestries. Liberman's wall hangings are not tapestries, but works done with appliqué of cloth upon cloth, often with linoleum block printing to create figurative images on the surface.

An obvious uniqueness of Liberman's work is her approach to the Holocaust using maps. The maps provide the viewer with a sense of where the drama of the Shoah unfolded, how it changed from event to event, and is mixed with documentation which allows the Holocaust Wall Hangings to function not only as aesthetically interesting works but also as monumental educational tools. The approach to the Holocaust via maps presents a stark realization of the extent of Nazi destruction and how the Shoah is unlike forms of contemporary genocide. While Bosnia, for example, witnessed genocidal destruction and mass rape of women, it took place, despite all of its horror, in a very small part of Europe. The Holocaust, by comparison, witnessed hunts for Jews from the Atlantic ocean to the Volga River, from the North Sea to the Mediterranean. Liberman's EUROPE 1945 affirms the scale of destruction as it visually transmits the reality that Europe had became a cemetery for Jews. This wall hanging is another map with heaps of bodies everywhere. Lest the viewer not have a frame of reference, most of the works are surrounded with some text providing both a title and understanding of the event, much in the style of eighteenth and nineteenth century Broadsides.

In addition, the Holocaust Wall Hangings also provide what may be called an aerial perspective on the Europe of the death camps, on the Amsterdam of Anne Frank, and on the geometry of the death camps themselves. One might speculate that utilization of this perspective as an artistic device is an inadvertent homage to Liberman's husband, Robert Liberman, who flew with the American Army Air Corps. This perspective is not new, but it is new in art about this subject. During the war, the Luftwaffe made aerial photographs of all the killing centers, death camps and concentration camps in their various stages of development. During varying periods of World War II, more specifically after the spring of 1944, the British and Americans took aerial reconnaissance photos over Auschwitz, Buchenwald, Dachau, Bergen Belsen and other camps. These original photographs are found in the National Archives in Washington. Another American artist, Arie Galles from New Jersey, embarked in the last few years on a project based upon aerial perspectives of the death camps, executed in charcoal and accompanied with poems by Jerome Rothenberg. So, while Liberman's wall hangings are cartographic, the viewer is not above the emotion of the events, which the artist spells out in their enormity with sewn-on and printed statistics, rail cars, concentration camp blocks, and the like. What Liberman adds, moreover, is a vision of blood on the soil through her artistic use of red beads sewn into the body of her work.

The color field used in most of Liberman's work is dominated by the Nazi colors—red, black and white. The use of these colors, also used by Russian Constructivists, is a reminder of how the Nazi leadership not only manipulated words to deter victims from knowing of their true fate, but also manipulated color to produce power. Liberman, on the other hand, uses the same colors as an act of subversion, to expose within those color elements a history of destruction.

Liberman also utilizes some subtle means to tell the Holocaust story. KRISTALLNACHT shows a map of Germany with the fiery places of destruction against Jews and Jewish property of November 9–10, 1938, what some regard as a rehearsal for the final solution. But in this work, while Germany, and hence the question of German guilt, emerges strongly, the cartographic outline of the rest of Europe is scarcely visible, suggesting the meekness of response before the beginning of World War II. WANNSEE PLANS is a black and white fabric map of Europe, evoking the "uniforms" of camp inmates, on which are block printed skulls. The artist tersely repeats what was announced in secrecy—the future numbers of destruction from the infamous meeting of January 20, 1942, which confirmed plans set in motion as early as June 1941, for "the final solution of the Jewish question."

Not all of Liberman's wall hangings deal with maps. Her PLAN OF AUSCHWITZ-BIRKENAU is reminiscent of an architect's drawing, with significant buildings, rail spur, gas chambers and crematoria laid out with geometric exactness. Sections of the camp are numbered and annotated. The physical size of this piece, 97×109 inches, is suggestive of the massiveness of this killing center, which consumed more than a million lives. ROAD TO AUSCHWITZ details the major rail links, with a multitude of railroad freight cars block-printed over the map of Europe.

While Liberman's narratives might be called episodic, the nature of her choice of subject raises questions that are important in connecting the historical and visual. In this case, it is an artistic representation that provides the impulse for intellectual inquiry. Thus, one might ask, what created the basis for the spatial geometry and immensity of the camp of Auschwitz? From viewing PLAN OF AUSCHWITZ-BIRKENAU, the viewer might reflect on the importance of railroad technology and that Germany might have won the war had it not had such an obsession with using the means of transportation to move Jews to points of destruction rather than send provisions to the front line fighting forces.

Part of Liberman's work focuses on the life of Anne Frank. She is Hitler's most famous victim, a known symbol, which places more of a creative burden on an artist who wishes to use her as a model. Each of Liberman's works suggests a specific emotion. ANNE FRANK'S HIDING PLACE, for example, suggests through image and text, the claustrophobia of hiding. ANNE FRANK'S AMSTERDAM is a spider web-like map of the canalled city superimposed on multiple small photos of Anne Frank. This is suggestive of how the history of Amsterdam has been altered because of Miep Gies's accidental discovery of the Diary after the Frank family was deported. Anne Frank is now associated with the city where she had so many hopes and was betrayed. Is the artist asking, in this work, about how many more Anne Franks there were in hiding? And she is certainly providing homage to the million and a half Jewish children who perished.

For those who prefer to diminish the Jewish aspects of Anne Frank's character, and believe, as she wrote before deportation, that things would turn out all right, Liberman's ANNE FRANK'S JOURNEY suggests the tragic ending of the story that most people know little about from reading only the Diary. Anne and her sister Margot were deported to Westerbork, in Eastern Holland, then to Auschwitz and finally to Bergen Belsen, where she perished under terrible conditions. Liberman's rendition of this on fabric suggests the immensity of the journey and its duration through repetition of images. As Anne Frank reaches Bergen Belsen, her image begins to fade. Indeed, how can we imagine the young girl who wrote her eloquent Diary succumbing in a place of typhus, mass starvation, tens of thousands of unburied bodies, and even cannibalism? Even the simple monument at Bergen Belsen suggests the problem as it proclaims: "Earth, Reveal Not the Blood Shed on Thee!"

One of Liberman's concluding panels, SIX MILLION, creates a European map from images of arms with numbers. However, the artist has not used tattoo numbers of actual victims, as some others have done, but has placed them in a way so as to signify the Jewish deaths in each country. The result is a landscape cluttered with arms, except for Switzerland. SIX MILLION, completed in 1988, might be different if done today, given changes in attitudes about Swiss neutrality and negotiations about Jewish assets and their return. Recently, a Swiss historian, commenting on Swiss complicity through its banking practices, concluded that "Auschwitz was also in Switzerland."

Not all of the Wall Hangings are based on maps of destruction. Some are simple vignettes, such as BOXCAR, which appears as a naively constructed boxcar with a photo of Anne Frank sewn onto the door. In an interesting way, the artist in this case reflects on the simple adaptation of technology for a deadly purpose, and at the same time gives us a feel for the loneliness and terror that accompanied deportation. FENCED IN provides a vision of inmates in a concentration camp. As they all look alike, in a deathly state, one is reminded of what philosopher Emil Fackenheim has said about the distinctiveness of the Nazi camps—the appearance of the *musselman*, the walking dead. Fackenheim asks a question which may underlie some of Liberman's thought on the Holocaust—where would Jesus of Nazareth have been in 1942 and could he and his family, Jews by conventional and Nazi definition, have become *musselmanders*? That question has a speculative answer, as Jesus did not live in the twentieth century. However, events similar to the Holocaust have occurred in Bosnia, Rwanda, and other locations, and *FENCED IN* might now easily be interpreted in a different way if exhibited in Sarajevo.

But the uniqueness of the Holocaust compared to other events is repeated over and over again in Liberman's wall hangings. *TWO THOUSAND YEARS* is a work that identifies Jewish Diaspora communities in Europe that were obliterated by the Germans. The dominant symbol is a red "Lion of Judah" used in the border of the wall hanging and printed inverted in white where communities vanished. This piece might have some resonance to Native Americans/First Peoples whose civilization of several thousand years disappeared in the Western Hemisphere after the arrival of Columbus. Indeed, the number of Native Americans who died by disease and sword is estimated to be around ninety million people. So what makes the Holocaust different and so worthy of this artist's attention? The answer is found in the narrative of the Holocaust Wall Hangings—the systematic and technologically-based killing that embraced the thought and actions of politicians, military and police groups, bureaucrats, and the corporations that built and helped operate the technology. The event took place against a group which had been emancipated and viewed as equal for more than a hundred years. Thus,

some reflection on Liberman's work raises the question that perhaps cannot be answered: "Why did it happen?" And the second, more important question, is: "Can it happen again?"

Liberman also pays attention to other groups victimized by the Nazi regime. The *FATE OF THE GYPSIES* is a testament to the Roma and Sinti peoples, a group perceived to be further on the margins of European society before the war, whose fate vis-à-vis the law was not altered much after the defeat of Germany. It is now believed that more than half a million members of the Roma and Sinti communities were killed on a racial basis. New evidence about this destruction has materialized even in the mid-1990s, especially at archeological excavations at the Concentration Camp Lety in the Czech Republic. This figure of 500,000 Gypsy victims may rise after more research is completed.

Lest hopelessness be left holding the upper hand, Liberman also provides, in *REVOLT*, visual testaments to Jewish rebellions within the camps and ghettos, and another work, *JEWISH SERVICEMEN*, is a recognition that Jews in Allied armies fought the Nazis. But there should not be a misconception about intent. While it was well known that Nazi Germany was evil, the general public was essentially deprived of information about the camps until they were liberated from the end of 1944 through the spring of 1945. It is out of the memory of loss that Liberman hopes contemporary humanity can establish an initiative to react to ongoing forms of genocide.

Many people who encounter the Holocaust and understand the enormous loss to humanity and the Jewish people respond with the cliché, "Never Again." As we begin a new century, it is useful to reflect that "Never Again" does not mean too much, except for the Jewish people, who, through the State of Israel, now have a defensive system which did not exist in 1933 or during the years of the Holocaust. But "Never Again" didn't have much significance to the people of Bosnia, Rwanda, East Timor, and other places where genocide has become a more recurrent device for solving territorial and racial questions.

If the viewer's response to Liberman's Holocaust Wall Hangings is merely sorrow, then the artist may not have fulfilled her task. However, if the viewer understands that man's inhumanity to man persists, with anti-Semitism and racism being among the longest forms of prejudice, one may emerge with an understanding that civilization is defined in part by a constant struggle against such demonological forces. If this is acknowledged, then Liberman's art may indeed have an important role in healing the world.

Symbols and Signs of Longing in the Holocaust Wall Hangings of Judith Weinshall Liberman

by

Salvatore Scalora

In a large room with dimly lighted ceiling lamps, certain dark tapestries hang against walls, dozens of messengers from the Holocaust created by Israeli born artist Judith Liberman. This ambitious major body of work is divided into two spheres: the *Scenes of the Holocaust* and the *Maps of the Holocaust.* As a separate part of the whole, each banner is a chart, a transmitter of terrible memorabilia, seductive on the one hand because of its homespun material nature and horribly cryptic in its delivery of facts and figures on the other hand. If your human antenna is operating, you will not be spared this emotional visitation with the ghosts of the Holocaust. Joined together are images that portray the martyrs and heroes as well as the victims and their murderers, all set within the stage of World War II history. Judith Liberman, like all good, socially committed artists, has set a table before us. She hopes the encounter will leave an indelible mark. Even as a young ten year old living with her family in Israel during the war years, Liberman remembers that "the grim news was everywhere; it was in the air we breathed and it became part of us."

Decades later, these works are the mature expression of artist Judith Liberman, who has never forgotten the horror of the grim news of World War II. She has labored for years on this singular project, which has taken on a dramatic importance in her life, a personal cause to speak out about using the vehicle of visual art. Utilizing the traditional materials of fabric sewing, purchasing yards of commercially printed background cloth, selecting specialty metallic surfaced textiles and threads, she has combined these with other nontraditional techniques such as block printing and photocopied vinyl transfers of historical images. The wall hangings mix and blend various fragments that the artist freely assembles into large-scale fabric collages. Liberman has slowly birthed each tapestry, one at a time.

Floating on fields of shadowy backgrounds, the Holocaust Wall Hangings exist in states of contrast, chillingly modest and domestic in material formula and yet grand and expansive in concept. Even the title of the series, the Holocaust Wall Hangings, seems to play at contrast. On one hand, it is a direct naming of the material format and yet it also alludes to a macabre tinged image of murders, *hangings*, accomplished with the use of rope. The colors of black, red, and gray create an ambiance of suffering, death and despair. Augmentations of metallic threads of silver enact a solemnness of purpose, of honor and respect, of duty and pride. Through the repeated patterns, colors, and shapes and designs of memory, we are all drawn, coaxed to explore the depths, the Netherworld of the Nazi hatred machine, exposed here as a grave, dark purgatory. The ironically named *GIFTGAS* is here as well.

Judith Liberman is intent to keep the ashes of the Holocaust smoldering for all the world to see through the vehicle of her art. "*We must not forget what has happened.*" She speaks to us. As a woman seamstress, she has cut the cloth and sewn the boundaries securely. As an artist, she has immersed herself in the darkness of the Holocaust's tragic legacy, Hitler's plan to end the "Jewish problem" through total genocide. In show-and-tell fashion, the scenes and maps each reveal their carefully metered share of Liberman's memorial series. Deftly, the artist has co-opted the form of Hitler's hanging banners, the empirical signage of the Third Reich, into her own style of social response.

Some of the most powerful map images are those dedicated to Anne Frank. One of the most notable works reveals several dozen gray, ghost-like images of her. This particular wall hanging is titled *ANNE FRANK'S AMSTERDAM*.

But unlike what the title of this work suggests, this particular World War II era Amsterdam is no longer Anne Frank's alone. Gazing at and through the overlaid spider web tangle of Amsterdam's city streets, we, the present day viewers who are confronted with Anne Frank's depicted memory, are ironically both separated from the child martyr by this symbolic grillwork and also magnetically drawn into it, like bees to nectar. Here we hover for a certain borrowing of time. We stand transfixed, suspended in an act of social acknowledgment of *the dead Anne Frank*. We are facing a demonstration of the symbolization of good and evil, of the riddles of cause and effect that are layered and represented here. The aerial map of Amsterdam's street plan is transformed into an artistic metaphor for a net of imprisonment beneath which the gray, pallid, multiple portraits of Anne Frank lie as if detached and floating.

ANNE FRANK'S AMSTERDAM is certainly an emotionally loaded image. As audience, we are fed a visualization of this young Jewish child whose story is a touchstone in the history of the Holocaust. We may wonder how artist Judith Liberman conceives of this particular work, what her intention is. Is this work a "teaching device," like a large scale chart to unroll and hang up before a class? Or is it a commemorative banner, a beautifully crafted memorial marker? The answer lies, to a great degree, in the issue of artistic intent and context in contemporary art. Within the walls of a gallery or museum, the Holocaust Wall Hangings are expressions of art, the fruitful end product of a creative process that seeks generally to communicate with audiences. All artists seek engagement, introspection, and thoughtful questioning from their audiences. There are rarely fixed points that must be ingested before savoring a work of art. You come before it as you are, full of your own identity, cultural markings, and life experiences. The aesthetic experience may be unique to each and every viewer in fact.

Though this image of young Anne Frank has the potential to reach out to everyone, it seems to me to be especially important that young adults and children view this work and the others created in her memory. There is a lesson here that Anne Frank and the artist share with us. The lesson is that the child Anne Frank's only "crime" was to be a Jew. For that alone, she and six million other Jews were exterminated by Nazi Germany. We are facing a visualization, a symbolization of Anne Frank, a child like any other except that she has the dubious honor of being a casualty, a fallen martyr, a victim of the world's most diabolical crimes against humanity. Overdone? No, I don't think so. The history of the Holocaust is there behind these works. Liberman, the artist, seems to be carefully saying, "Never forget the child Anne Frank, because now you are a witness as well."

Judith Liberman's overriding presence can be felt everywhere in these wall hangings; her handwork is crude at times and elegant at other times. In the face of such emotive subject matter, it seems irrelevant to examine the interplay between artistic expression and craft construction. *Where we get to* is ultimately more absorbing than *how we get there*. Her choices in materials, design and construction are all aspects of her formal decisions that facilitate the process of expression making.

Without a single doubt, the Holocaust Wall Hangings are artistic expressions that present interesting challenges to consuming audiences. One must consider that the artist offers these works as a Jewish woman who both speaks for herself and for an unspecified community of other Jews as well. The reception within Jewish and non-Jewish audiences to these works may present interesting results. For instance, even within the Jewish community, those families that have lost relatives to the Holocaust may react differently by degree than those who did not, and certainly the reaction of Jews who survived the Holocaust is a further possible variation of intensity. Reception by Israeli Jews may be different from that of Jews who live in the U.S. The Holocaust Wall Hangings are by no means

only addressed to Jews. The events of the Holocaust are universal tragedies of unparalleled human scale. Liberman's expressions are for the consumption of anyone who cares about the issue of cultural genocide.

This body of work's teaching capacity is compatible with the history of politically based art. In these cases, the artist functions more as a community or social leader and teacher-advocate than a solo artist who speaks to more private concerns. Does this in any way diminish the more traditional aspect of regarding the Holocaust Wall Hangings as a form of "true fine art"? Not at all. There are countless examples in the history of art of artists who explored humanistic subjects even before the category of political art came to be. The wall hangings have artistic pedigree and sit squarely within the accepted boundaries of contemporary artistic expressions; in fact, they can move within various circles of focus in their exhibition life. Because of Judith Liberman's Holocaust Wall Hangings and other works like them, it is unlikely that the Holocaust will ever see a diminished interest in the area of academic study or in the arts.

Let us briefly look at the general audience's role and function in the life of the Holocaust Wall Hangings. As willing participants, the audience members become the vessels, the human recipients of certain informational and emotional cargoes that lie rooted within the work. They need not be expected to support the type of work that is embodied in literature or historical writing. Art is a distillation of words and knowledge that, when properly orchestrated, can create engagement and dialogue, and can provide opportunity for transference in the audience, perhaps even transcendence. This process of audience digestion is common to all situations. While we could safely say that all creative works want to unload themselves on their audiences, to reveal their inner selves to their audiences, it is particularly true in the case of these socially haunting works. They, more so than any other form, seek release. We as audiences are the witnesses, the sponges of soulfulness that the artist hopes will carry away a blend of knowledge and emotional reaction.

As audience, we should remember the image of Anne Frank long after we directly experience the wall hangings dedicated to her. Though she was only one of the millions of Jews to be shot, starved, and exterminated by the Nazis, it is nevertheless a fact that *she is the one whose words survive in literature*. Over time, Anne Frank has achieved a profound but unfortunate status as one of the immortals of the Holocaust, a primal symbolization of its horror.

In another wall hanging, ANNE FRANK'S HIDING PLACE, Anne writes that she "wanders from one room to another, downstairs and up again, feeling like a songbird whose wings have been clipped and who is hurling himself in utter darkness against the bars of his cage." Surely it is undeniable that Anne Frank's story of her family's self-imposed captivity to escape Nazi detection is one of the most poignant pieces of literature to have survived the Holocaust. Here Liberman treats the image and text so directly, duplicated and encased in a wire-like grid. If we look closely, there is an undeniable resemblance between the artist and our Anne Frank. Liberman has a flair for dramatic moments and uses text and image advantageously in order to increase the emotional ties that the audience may feel in this work. Ultimately, we must not overlook one very critical fact: The Holocaust Wall Hangings are a creative and personal link to the suffering of the Jews of the Holocaust for their creator, Judith Liberman, who lived out the war as a child safely in Israel. Her connectedness is not by way of her immunity to its physical horror, but by her cultural and psychological experience of it.

In connecting to Liberman's Anne Frank, we find ourselves involved in more than just the gaze of Anne Frank. Her image and words evoke a deep soulful sense of *longing* in me. What is it? The dictionary says that longing is a yearning or a great desire. But it fails to mention the longing of the heart, that blood organ that lies at the center of our body which is also the embodiment of our core of emotions and feelings. Does longing of the heart cause pain and produce tears? Should we ask a medical doctor who deals with the physical realm to answer a question of a spiritual nature? No. It is better to turn to our own experience to seek out this sense of longing. We humans mourn our dead in ways that transcend both realms. Our very cells are repositories of memory, especially sadness or trauma. How do we long for our dead mothers? Our fathers? A brother or sister? Our spouses? Our friends? In acts and experiences of longing, we belong to ourselves, our family and friends. We are lodged in this world, set within our own lives. Belonging and longing are both about love and connection to something very deeply rooted.

My own experience tells me that longing is most often manifested as a sense of incompleteness, of inexplicable loss; in extreme situations, it is a psychic ransacking, which may never yield recovery. The living long for the dead, as we also often long for childhood, even for our country and our culture of origin. We mark the passage of our own lives with the stones of our losses.

As an artist, Judith Liberman presents us with fabric wall hangings that are simple to visually read in some cases and very complex and strange in others. The Holocaust Wall Hangings are related to all art that seeks a social dialogue, works as diverse as Pablo Picasso's *Guernica* painting, any of Sue Coe's illustrated books, or Alfredo Jaar's illuminating installations. The categories of subjects are particular to Liberman's own redemptive stylizations. She uses design, abstraction, figuration, text, historical documentary data, word labels, whatever works best. The entire series is completely unique. There is no other exactly like it in the world. I believe these works come from a special place in Judith Liberman's artistic career. It is, in my estimation, her principal legacy as a mature artist. They are masterworks, unmatchable poetic gifts of expression and feelings.

There are no easy routes to healing. The German nation, since the end of World War II, has struggled with its own demons in regard to the Holocaust. Today, the quest continues for a cleansing process, an understanding of historical events. Jews and Germans are tied together in this case. Both seek the same, but wounds are slow to heal. The process of healing is painful and lasts far longer than the actual trauma that caused the original wound. How will Germans look at the wall hangings? We can only triumph over our fears and pain when we can face them. There is nothing easy about it, not then and not now.

Liberman's maps are alluring from a distance and disarming upon a closer viewing. Because of their mostly encoded data, their terrible news is held in check, is charted away. One thing is certain in surveying the entire series of wall hangings: Liberman plays at many interesting strategies and uses of materials to work her messages. Sometimes with the eye of beauty, and sometimes with the eye of the beast, Liberman sews her surfaces with enticing visual lures. We face a certain horrible, dark beauty in all of Judith Liberman's wall hangings. Sumptuous of surface, rich in original fabric material, and flawlessly executed with layers of printed and appliquéd cloth pieces, the hanging fabric banners beckon to us and then deliver a certain inner sting, a dose of bitter medicine.

In some cases, the images portray the massive Nazi death devices. In some works, the systematic identification of Jews is the subject, highlighting the Nazi obsession with marking human prisoners and collecting "data." In some cases, we find that the maps reveal staggering levels of enemy aggression and victim retreat and escape routes. The viewing is a mixed menu. Sometimes the audience is facing an abstracted map and other times the audience faces fields of dismembered arms and hands. The Jewish heroes and fighters are represented as well and sometimes the stark black and white patterns of concentration camp prisoners bring the viewer's eyes to the rawness of suffering and despair.

One very disturbing banner is the one with hundreds of commercially printed, vinyl, historic photographs, appliquéd onto the surface, bringing a ghostly, documentary reality to bear. Another one presents the crematoria, medieval and diabolical, pitiless in their functionality. It would be impossible to even suggest that there is no emotional price to pay here, both for the maker and the viewer. Surely in the making of the wall hangings, Judith Liberman faced the demons of history and transcribed them into a personal visual interpretation that she could live with. For instance, theatrical or not, the black iron doors of the red flaming incinerator chambers are the devil's devices and picturing them is no easy task, not even decades after the end of World War II. The representation of these death chambers is solemn: They represent both the attempted and the achieved annihilation of millions of Jews.

Judith Liberman has balanced many concerns in creating her series: her personal feelings regarding the Holocaust, her artistic studio-based explorations that helped her give voice to those feelings, and ultimately her concerns in attempting to reach out to and communicate with a wide audience. Throughout, Liberman handles it all with a very strong sense of herself as both the creator and also an individual Jew, a witness and a voice against the Holocaust's legacy of torture and death.

Liberman envisions the lines that permeate her banners, always the white lines, to represent the long thin lines of humanity, waiting. The lines are repeated in the prisoners' suits and the horizontal boards of the barracks and the rails of the trains. Grayish, darkly printed railroad boxcars cross the midnight velvet fields of the wall hangings. German style lettering places the Holocaust in the belly of the European continent. Checkered backgrounds grid and cage the sewn-over visual data as well as present a detached graph-like view that freezes levels of the inhumanity presented. The silhouette of Germany is a Black Forest timber wolf. Believe it. Believe the fear. The Lilliputian soldiers of the *EINSATZGRUPPEN* are the stuff of nightmares. The blood soaked, dismembered body dumps add weight to the mountain of loss and disfigurement of the global Jewish Diaspora. Skeletal bony hands reach out through girded wire fences. The appendages of the faceless Jews reach out to us. Do we dare touch them? Do we carry a heavy heart for them?

Would we dare substitute ourselves within their place? Who would treat human beings like this? Do such terrible things to them?

Ultimately, the road to redemption is lined with unpleasant truths. Artist Judith Liberman has dared to face her deeply rooted connection to the horrors of the Holocaust. She has processed these most difficult of events through the creative studio approach, and while the ghosts of the Jewish Holocaust will never leave Judith Liberman, I believe she has found some sense of peace for herself. Along with her acts of creation and process came moments of remembering and longing. Through her efforts, she has given us all a vital series of works which will continue to pay tribute to the memory of Jews dozens of decades beyond the new millennium. The Holocaust will never be forgotten.

Liberman's Holocaust Wall Hangings, Art and Jewish Art

by

Ori Z. Soltes

ONE

The human condition is fraught with paradox. If the God who we assume made us, with a purpose, is by definition unfathomable—His very *name* ineffable (beyond offering to us the fact that God *is*, for the Hebrew letters of the unpronounceable name *mean* "isness")—then is it any surprise that we, God's creatures, are laden with unfathomable contradictions? We can create the most majestic echoes of God's creation: music, poetry, dance, painting, sculpture. Yet we, alone of all species, turn that creative inclination not merely to destructive ends, but apply it to *entertaining* ourselves with the most intense and extraordinary forms of hurting each other.

By further paradox, as words separate humanity from other species, extending us beyond where others reach, words are marvelously limiting. They obscure as well as clarify; they tie down as well as liberate. Visual art offers one among several other media which humans have uniquely at our disposal in our attempt to understand the universe and ourselves, when words fail.

In the Jewish tradition, it has often been thought that visual self-expression would contradict the purposes of God—that the Second Commandment proscribes image-making. It doesn't, of course—it only proscribes the making of images for the purposes of worship; it prohibits mistaking them for gods—and across Jewish history and geography there have been as many times and places rich with visual self-expression as there have been those where it has been inhibited. Indeed, were not the experience of Jews so often one of expulsion and destruction, no doubt more would have been made and surely more would have

17

survived as evidence of what was visually expressed by Jews.

Certainly as the twentieth century began to unfold, in cultural capitals like Paris and Berlin and London—even in Prague, Vienna, Budapest and St. Petersburg—Jews began to explode as a contributing part of the visual life that would become the modernist painting, sculpture, and architecture of our era. Names like Pissarro, Israels, Liebermann, Ury, Romberg, Antokolski, Levitan, to say nothing of Chagall, Modigliani, Soutine, and Lipschitz are among those associated with the varied directions taken by painting and sculpture even before World War I had covered the European landscape with darkness.

No moment in human experience reveals the dark side of humanity more profoundly than does the Holocaust that followed a generation later. And no experience has provoked a more elaborate and continuous outpouring of attempts to grasp its unfathomability than the Holocaust has. No group was more aware of the twistability of words to say the opposite of what they mean than were the Nazis, who were masters of manipulating words. And since that horrendous era, billions and billions of words have explored what cannot be effectively explained.

So, too, and ironically enough, even as the Holocaust destroyed so much of the modernist world for Jews and non-Jews alike, it neither managed to exterminate Jews and Judaism nor did it eliminate the burgeoning of a variety of forms of Jewish visual self-expression. Indeed, as the world of seeing shifted its center toward New York by the end of the 1940s, a multitude of Jews played roles in shaping the art of the second half of our century—and continue to do so.

And nearly every Jewish artist active since the Catastrophe has felt the need, sooner or later to respond to its traumatic detritus. And so what we speak of as "Holocaust Art"—by which I mean any form of visual response to the Holocaust, created during or after it, by anybody, Jew or non-Jew—is, by paradox and irony, one of the most fruitful forms of art, *particularly* by Jews, in the past fifty years. The darkness that Hitler spread over the world has yielded, among other forms of unexpected light, a wealth of troubled and troubling visual efforts at grasping the unfathomable.

In the last two decades in particular, with ever-increasing speed, the range of forms of visual self-expression with regard to the Holocaust has extended towards infinity. Survivors and the children of survivors, Jews and also non-Jews—sometimes, especially, Germans—have wrestled with a limitless range of trying to respond in non-verbal, visual terms to the unique effort of the Nazis to torture and destroy.

TWO

Judith Weinshall Liberman's work falls gently and emphatically into this complex matrix of issues. She is part of the sweeping wave of Jews that has overwhelmed the shores of western art in this century for whom, *as* Jews, an implicit pair of questions has been: How do I as a Jewish artist fit into the history of western art—which for the past sixteen centuries has been largely Christian art? And what should be the sources of visual inspiration from which I draw, coming from a tradition that has a reputation for being non-visual and certainly non-representational?

She is also one of the many to feel the unavoidable need to address the most horrendous period in Jewish—perhaps in human—history in her own unique visual terms. She is one of the fortunate, whose immediate family left Europe long before Hitler devoured it—but one of those who could not be untouched by that act of cannibalism, whether as a child hearing the constant news of its spreading circle of terror, or as an adult contemplating the far-flung crags and boulders of its moraine. The ripples of unfathomability impelled her to consider new means of visualization to help grasp the horror. We see this in the alternation of concrete, figurative representation—the faces of people and the shapes of boxcars—and what amounts to abstraction. For in their infinitizing quality, in their being too much and too many for the mind to really grasp, the maps and place-names and numbers acquire a distinctly abstract quality.

And if one of the questions of Jewish and general twentieth-century art is that of where to draw the line between figurative and abstract, Liberman has responded by hovering *on* that line. Abstraction persists in the diagonal lines of toy-soldier-figures over the amorphous fragments of what is a map or repeated lion images imprinted over the dotted lines of the abstract European geo-political landscape or repeating miniature boxcar images or simply a matrix of horizontal and vertical lines—superimposed over or interspersed with that very familiar figurative image: the face of Anne Frank.

The child in Liberman, recalling the child she was when she heard the first radio reports of Nazi progress, is drawn to that precocious child whose diary makes us weep with its splendid voice and the realization both that the voice was silenced so early and that over a million children like Anne Frank were silenced before they could speak. The traumatist in Liberman sees endless children, endless Anne Franks, endless boxcars, endless arms tattooed with numbers—endless lions as Lions of Judah whose roars have been silenced.

We also see her response as one of intentional paradox in the combination of materials that comprise her Holocaust Wall Hangings. The artist paints and prints and calligraphizes and stencils on sewn, appliquéd, embroidered and beaded textiles, not on the traditional and expected wood or canvas or paper. Soft, warm fabric is the medium used to recall the hardest, coldest extended moment in twentieth-century experience. Textiles are traditionally the kind of material used to shape the doorways into the Torah, center of Jewish ritual life throughout history: mantle, binding, *parokhet* (ark curtain). Such works have, over the centuries and across the Jewish world, tied the individual and the family to the community, as the numerous dedicatory inscriptions on them often attest. In a more generalized sense, fabric ordinarily shapes the comfort level of the spaces at home on which we walk and in which we sit and lie, awake and asleep, and defines the garments that embrace our very bodies. In Liberman's deft hands, the caressing textile medium of continuity has become the medium for a message about dehumanization and the attempt to destroy continuity.

Thus the artist creates work which embodies paradoxes that are central to the Holocaust as well as tied to questions in the history of Jewish art and its proliferation in the twentieth century. What and how should it be? How should it be understood? The Holocaust Wall Hangings obliquely address the notion that we can never fully encapsulate Jewish art by simple references to style, subject, or symbol; nor to material, artist identity or purpose—as they speak simultaneously of both the vast human capacity for horror and destruction, and the possibility for human salvation.

She chooses, again and again, the colors of Purgatory as they are understood in the symbolism of Italian Renaissance (Christian) art: red and black. Blood and death in her re-vision lead not only to despair, but out of the Inferno toward some sort of redemption—or at least of *hope*, that "tomorrow, one year from now, ten years from now, a hundred years from now someone somewhere contemplating the work will be moved enough to look into his/her heart and resolve to be human."

Against the persistent purgatorial red and black, Anne Frank's face breathes an immortal humanity which has survived because it *must*—in part through such works as these. Moreover, the fact that these soft, harsh wall hangings are dedicated to the memory of the artist's father, as an ultimate symbol, in how he *was*, of what is best among humans; to the memory of her brother, who died fighting for Israel's independence at age twenty-one; and to the memory of her husband, who never forgot what he saw as a member of the United States liberating forces at Dachau; not only ties the personal to the universal. It reminds us of that ultimate other thread—memory—found within the complex word-and-image-woven tapestry that comprises the history of art, Jewish art, and human experience. And it offers us the uplifting realization that in the exercise of memory, which underlies both word and image, the ultimate paradox of the human condition becomes available to us. For through memory and works such as these, mortality may be transmuted into immortality of a particular and profound sort. Death itself may be overcome.

List of the Holocaust Wall Hangings

by category

INTRODUCTORY

Attribution	Dedication	Remembrance

MAPS

Anne Frank's Amsterdam	The Einsatzgruppen	Revolt
Anne Frank's Hiding Place	Europe 1945	Road to Auschwitz
Anne Frank's Hiding Place II	Fate of the Gypsies	Search for Safety
Anne Frank's Journey	Gypsies Too	Six Million
Auschwitz Evacuation	Jewish Servicemen in World War II	Two Thousand Years
Camps	Kristallnacht	Voyage of the St. Louis
Cross	Plan of Auschwitz-Birkenau	Wannsee Plans

SCENES

At the Wall	The Final Solution	Monuments
Belongings	Fire	Monuments II
Boarding	Giftgas	Race Defiler
Boxcar	The Hand	Showers
Bunks	Hands	Triangles
Bunks II	Hands Up	Wire Fence
Cart	Insignia	Yellow Star
Fenced In	Memorabilia	

EPILOGUE

Count the Stars	Images	Sight
Forsaken	Power	Supplication
Good and Evil	Praise	Vanished
Holocaust Artist	Prayer	Witness
ID	Righteous	

List of Plates

1. ANNE FRANK'S JOURNEY   *Maps of the Holocaust*   81" × 127"   1988

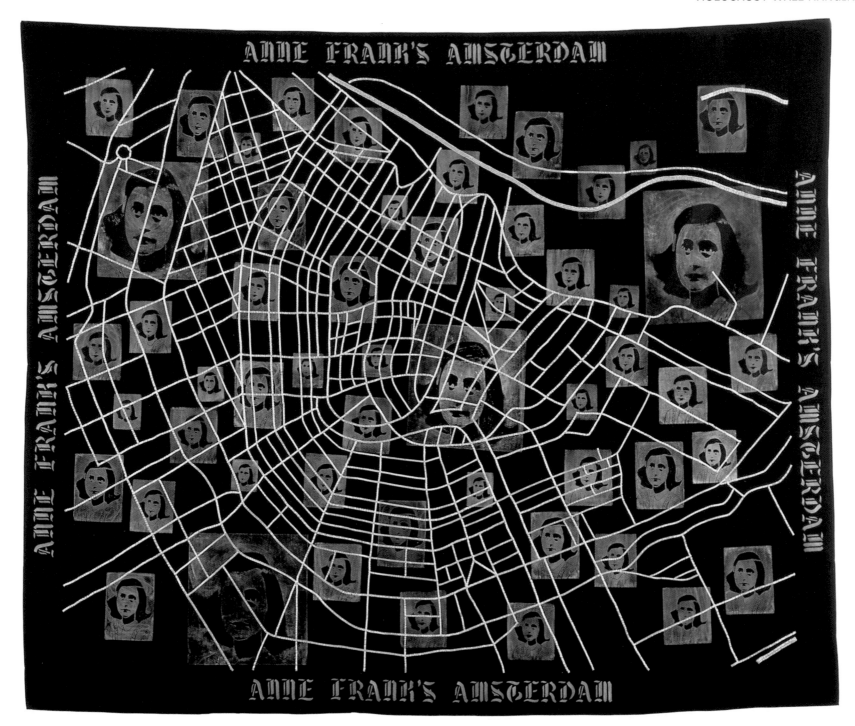

2. ANNE FRANK'S AMSTERDAM   *Maps of the Holocaust*   83" × 114"   1990

I wander from one room to another, downstairs and up again, feeling like a songbird whose wings have been clipped and who is hurling himself in utter darkness against the bars of his cage. "Go outside, laugh, and take a breath of fresh air," a voice cries within me, but I don't even feel a response any more; I go and lie on the divan and sleep, to make the time pass more quickly, and the stillness and the terrible fear, because there is no way of killing them.

3. ANNE FRANK'S HIDING PLACE   *Maps of the Holocaust*   67" × 106"   1989

4. REMEMBRANCE *Introductory*   62" × 93"   1989

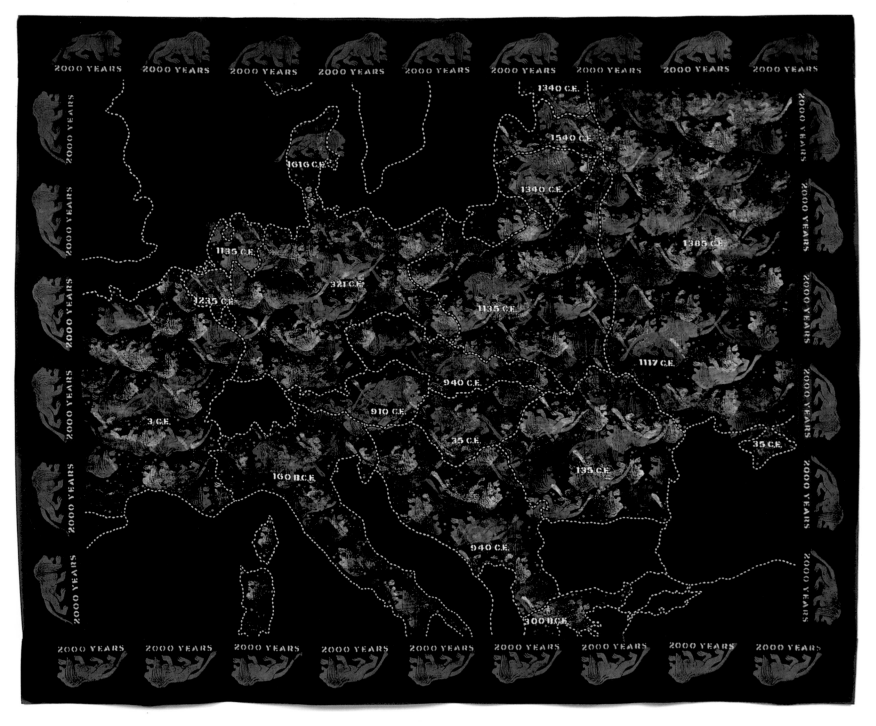

5. TWO THOUSAND YEARS *Maps of the Holocaust* 65" × 81" 1988

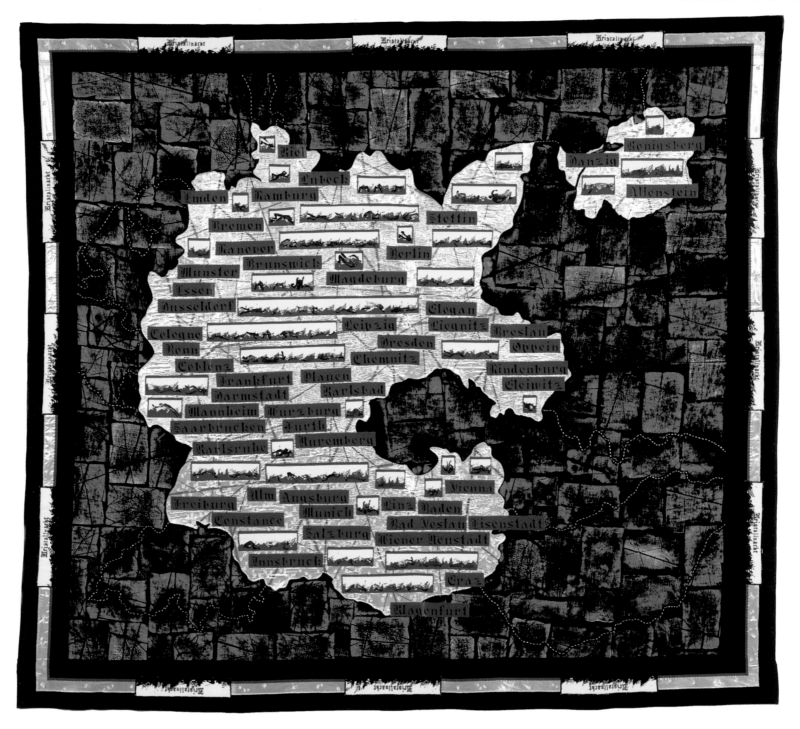

6. KRISTALLNACHT   *Maps of the Holocaust*   69" × 80"   1989

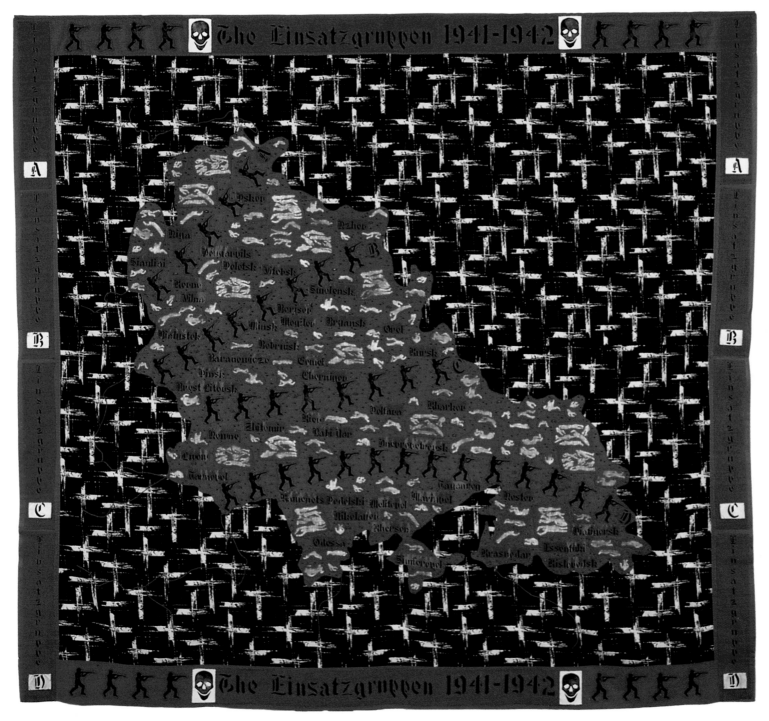

7. THE EINSATZGRUPPEN *Maps of the Holocaust* 86" × 96" 1990

8. WANNSEE PLANS   *Maps of the Holocaust*   64" × 84"   1988

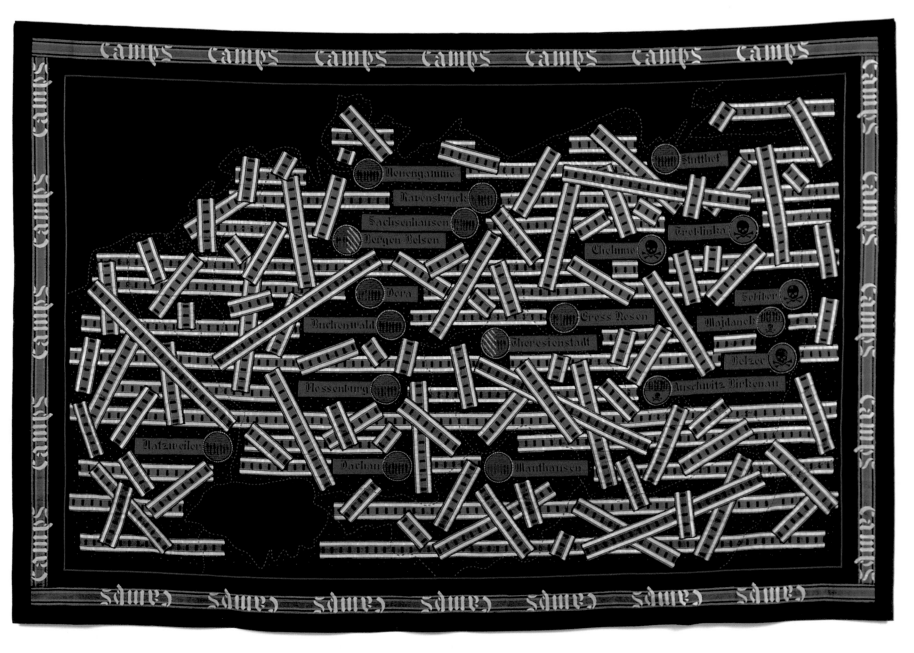

9. CAMPS *Maps of the Holocaust* 65" × 99" 1991

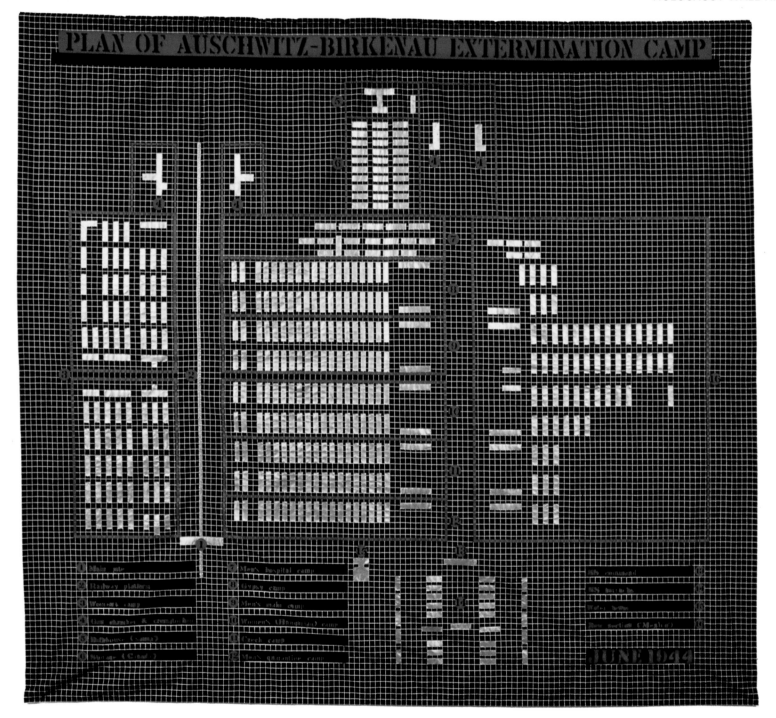

10. PLAN OF AUSCHWITZ-BIRKENAU   *Maps of the Holocaust*   97" × 109"   1991

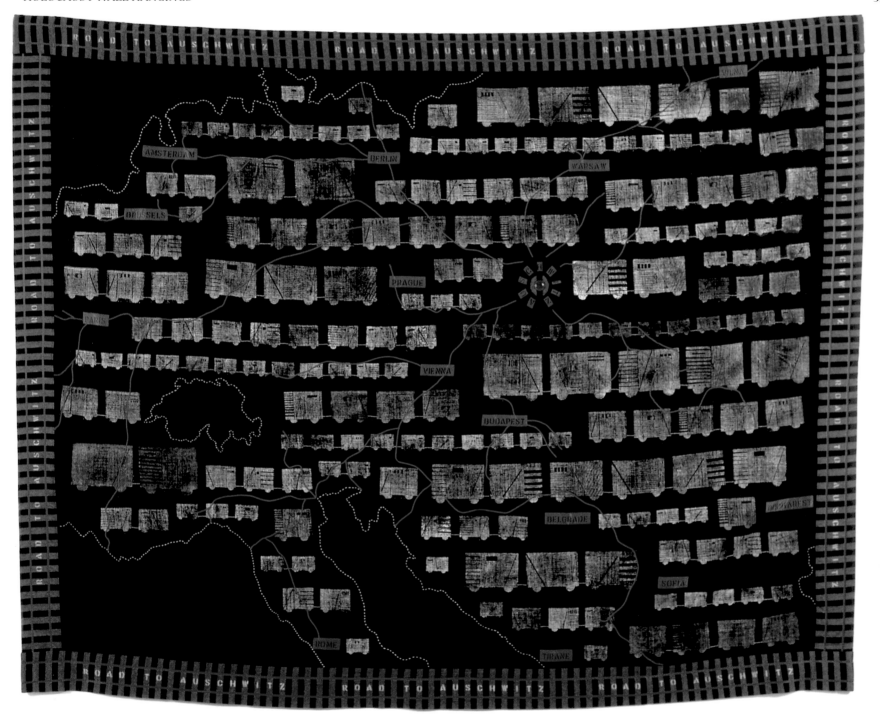

11. ROAD TO AUSCHWITZ *Maps of the Holocaust* 85" × 113" 1988

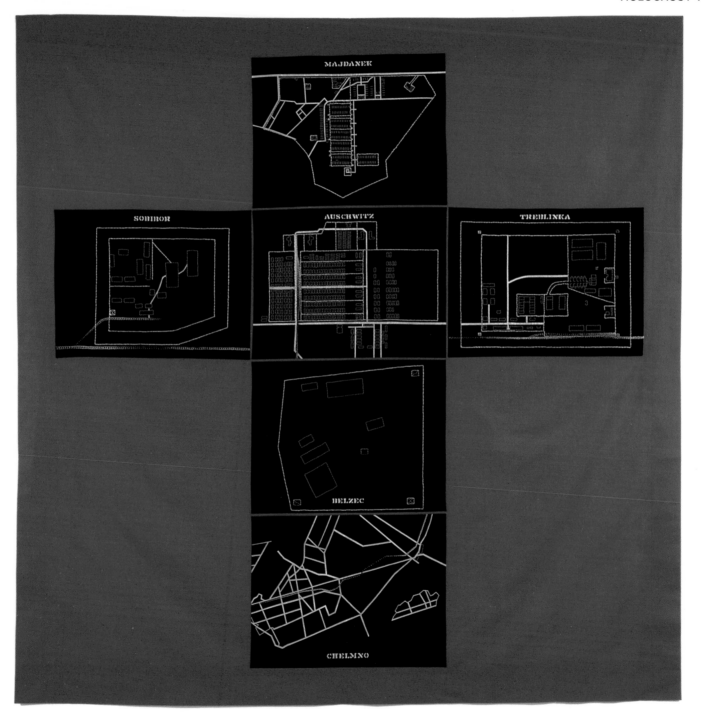

12. CROSS *Maps of the Holocaust* 81" × 81" 1996

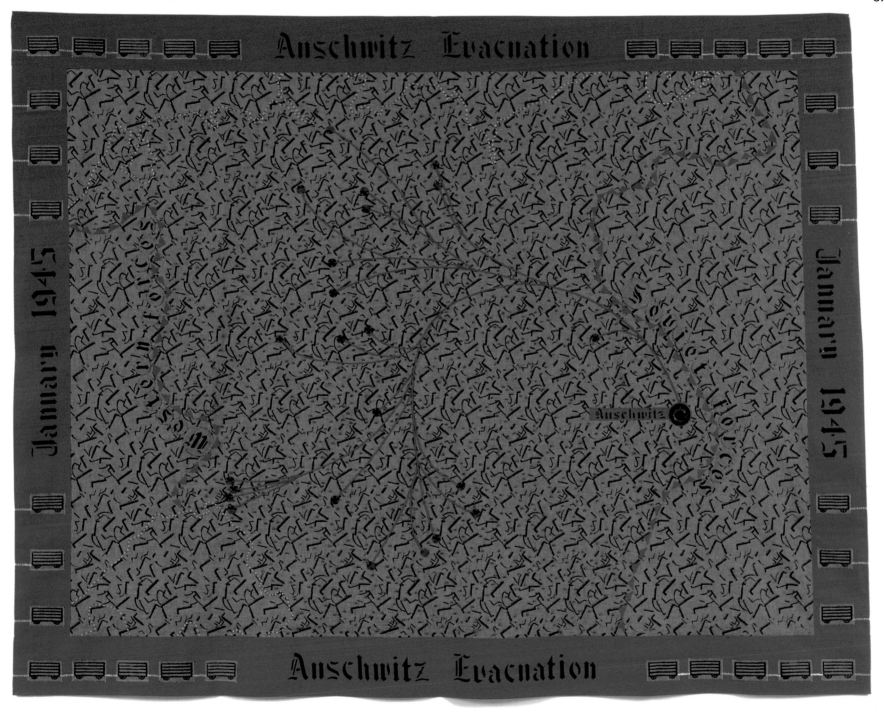

13. AUSCHWITZ EVACUATION *Maps of the Holocaust* 64" × 82" 1991

14. SIX MILLION   *Maps of the Holocaust*   72" × 81"   1988

15. FATE OF THE GYPSIES *Maps of the Holocaust* 62" × 80" 1990

16. EUROPE 1945   *Maps of the Holocaust*   85" × 112"   1988

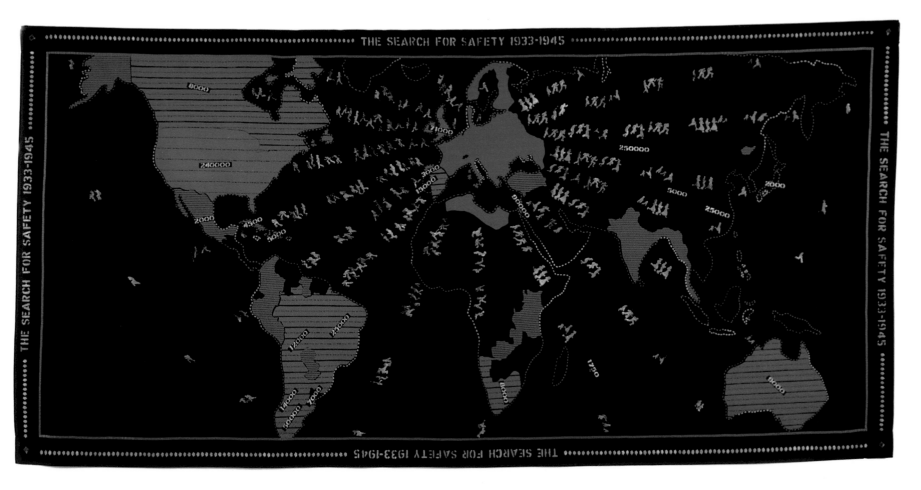

17. SEARCH FOR SAFETY *Maps of the Holocaust* 53" × 110" 1989

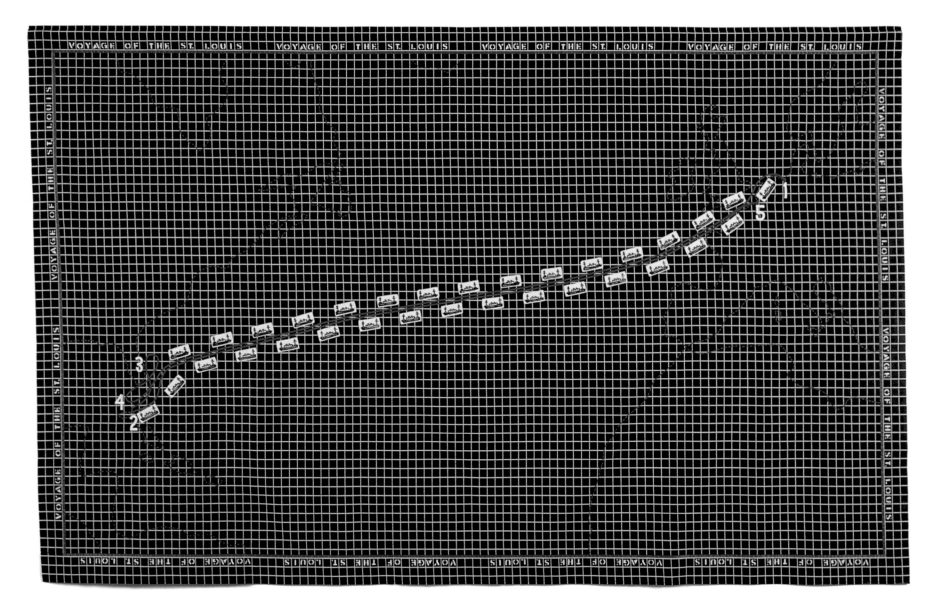

18. VOYAGE OF THE ST. LOUIS   *Maps of the Holocaust*   53" × 86"   1989

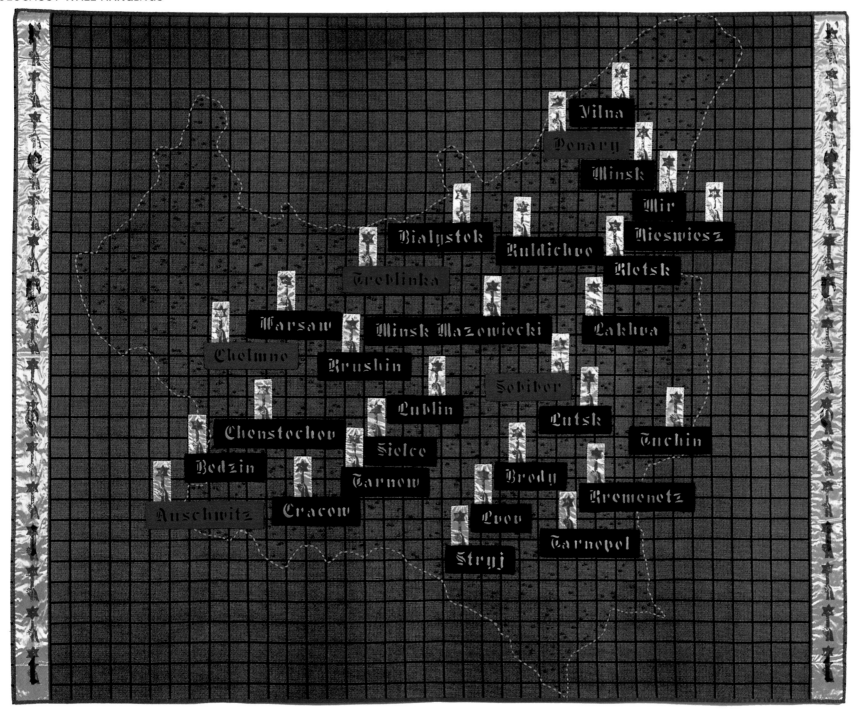

19. REVOLT *Maps of the Holocaust* 52" × 64" 1989

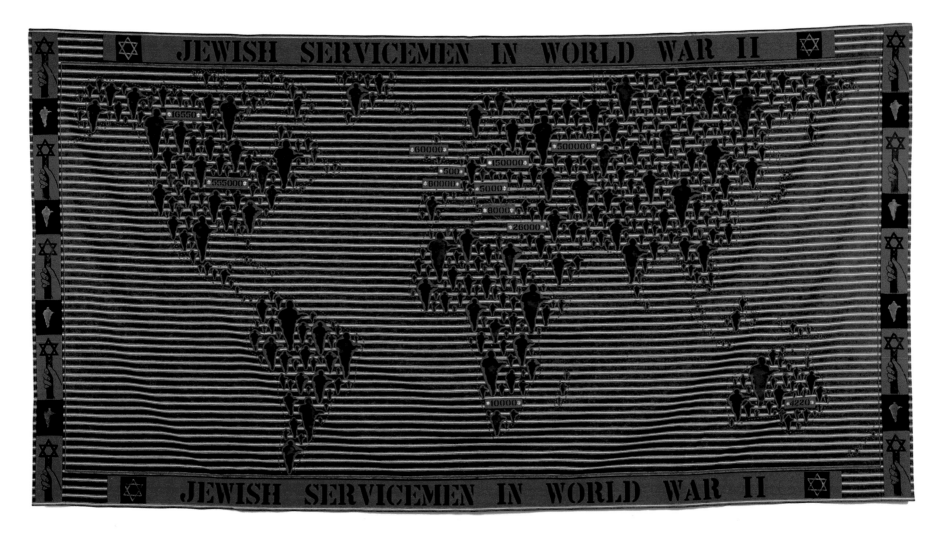

20. JEWISH SERVICEMEN IN WORLD WAR II   *Maps of the Holocaust*   57" × 110"   1991

21. HANDS UP   *Scenes of the Holocaust*   46" × 97"   1989

22. FENCED IN   *Scenes of the Holocaust*   48" × 137"   1989

23. CART   *Scenes of the Holocaust*   47" × 56"   1989

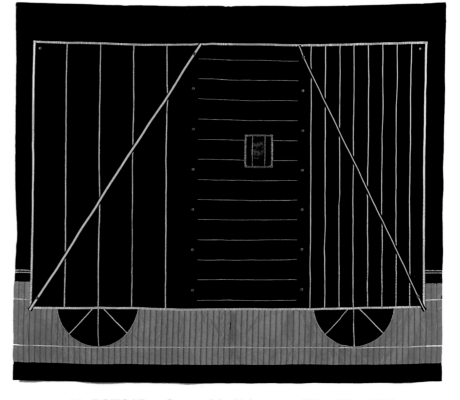

24. BOXCAR   *Scenes of the Holocaust*   75" × 88"   1991

25. BUNKS   *Scenes of the Holocaust*   23" × 56"   1989

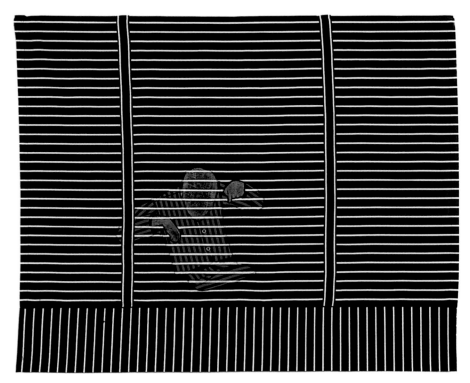

26. WIRE FENCE   *Scenes of the Holocaust*   45" × 58"   1989

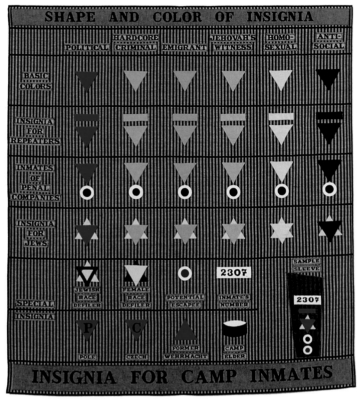

27. INSIGNIA   *Scenes of the Holocaust*   61" × 56"   1994

28. RACE DEFILER   *Scenes of the Holocaust*   44" × 21"   1998

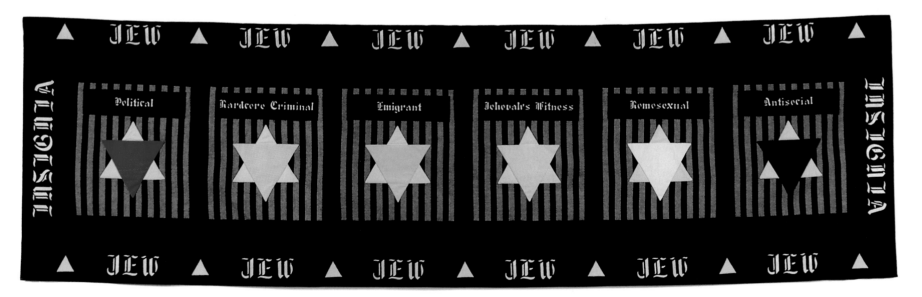

29. TRIANGLES   *Scenes of the Holocaust*   33" × 114"   1998

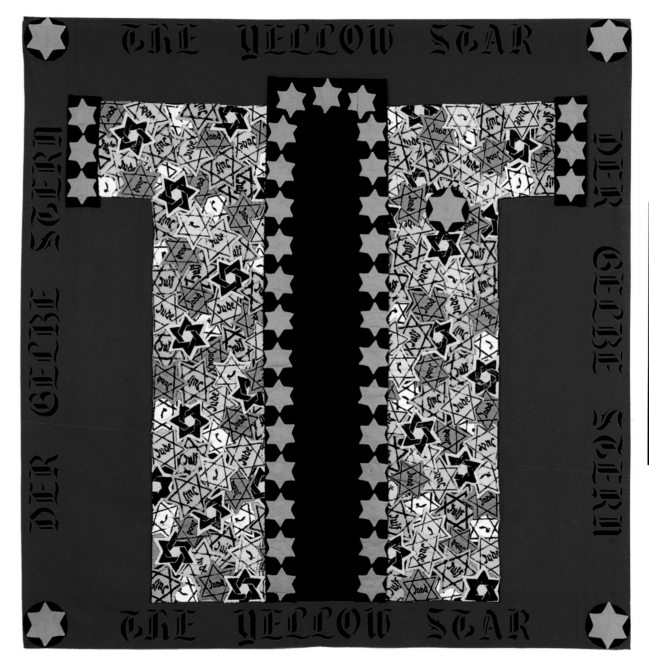

Detail

30. YELLOW STAR   *Scenes of the Holocaust*   51" × 51"   1994

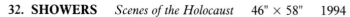

31. BOARDING *Scenes of the Holocaust* 46" × 58" 1994

32. SHOWERS *Scenes of the Holocaust* 46" × 58" 1994

Detail

Detail

33. GIFTGAS   *Scenes of the Holocaust*   42" × 48"   1994

Detail

34. THE FINAL SOLUTION *Scenes of the Holocaust* 67" × 67" 1990

35. FIRE   *Scenes of the Holocaust*   38" × 47"   1990

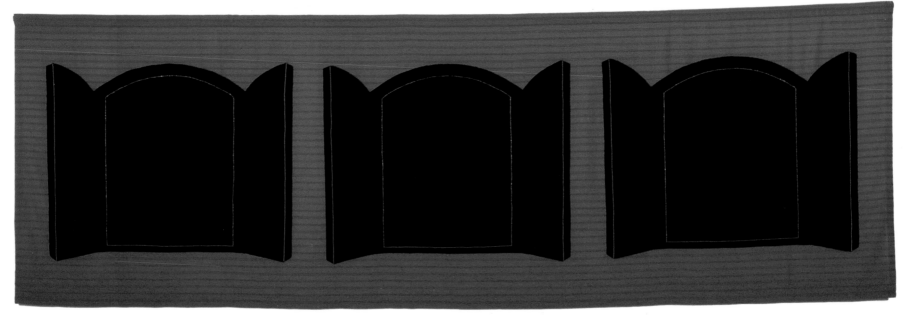

36. MONUMENTS   *Scenes of the Holocaust*   55" × 172"   1990

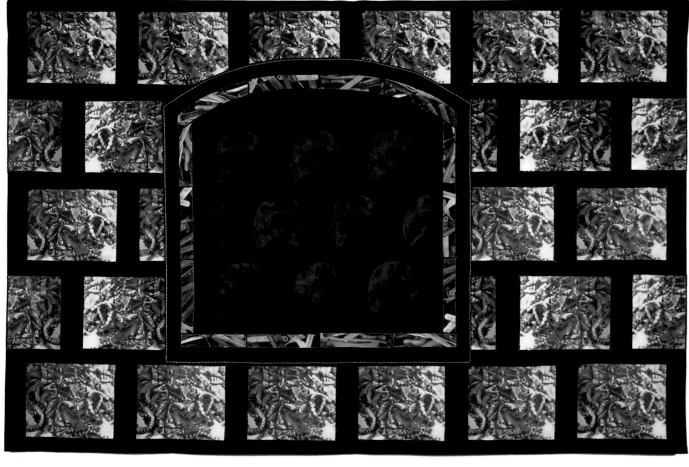

37. MEMORABILIA *Scenes of the Holocaust* 48" × 74" 1995

38. BELONGINGS *Scenes of the Holocaust* 25" × 130" 1995

Detail

39. GOOD AND EVIL   *Epilogue*   45" × 50"   1998

40. POWER *Epilogue* 21" × 51" 1999

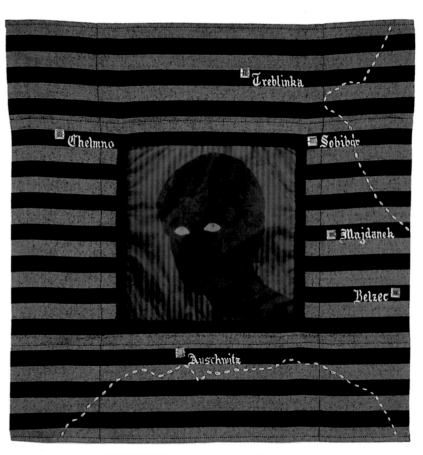

42. VANISHED *Epilogue* 21" × 21" 1998

41. PRAISE *Epilogue* 21" × 51" 1999

43. HOLOCAUST ARTIST   *Epilogue*   21" × 113"   1997

44. WITNESS   *Epilogue*   18" × 26"   1998

45. ID   *Epilogue*   21" × 26"   1998

Notes for Plates

1. ANNE FRANK'S JOURNEY
Maps of the Holocaust   81" × 127"   1988

In this map, we step beyond the building and city where Anne Frank hid during the Holocaust and see the long journey she was forced to travel during her short life. From her birthplace in Frankfurt, Germany, she fled with her family to Amsterdam, Holland. After hiding there from the Nazis, she was caught and sent to Westerbork, a transit camp in Holland, and from there to Auschwitz, Poland, and finally to Bergen Belsen, the concentration camp in Germany where she died. She was not yet sixteen when she died. In this map, her image, set against a backdrop of boxcars, becomes fainter as she nears her death at Bergen Belsen.

Both the images of the boxcars scattered over the background and Anne Frank's image along the path of her journey were block printed in silver acrylic on patches of fabric—burlap in the case of the boxcars, shiny synthetic for Anne Frank's likeness—which were then appliquéd on the black background fabric. The borders of the European countries were embroidered with gray cotton floss. The tracks representing Anne Frank's journey are rendered by means of a metallic silver ribbon, appliquéd and punctuated with faceted acrylic jewels. A metallic silver ribbon also forms the outline of train tracks along the border of the wall hanging, on which Anne Frank's image appears repeatedly, as if in motion.

2. ANNE FRANK'S AMSTERDAM
Maps of the Holocaust   83" × 114"   1990

The layout of the city of Amsterdam, where Anne Frank hid from the Nazis, evokes an image of a spider's web. This layout is here superimposed upon repeated images of Anne Frank. The repeated images allude to the picture-covered wall of Anne Frank's room.

The likeness of Anne Frank was carved in graduated sizes into linoleum blocks and printed on separate pieces of fabric, which were appliquéd onto the background fabric. The map of the city is made up of appliquéd silver ribbon, glistening like a spider's web. Anne Frank's image appears trapped in the web of the city.

3. ANNE FRANK'S HIDING PLACE
Maps of the Holocaust   67″ × 106″   1989

Superimposed upon an image of Anne Frank is a floor plan of the second and third floors of the annex of the building in Amsterdam where she and her family hid from the Nazis and where she wrote her now-famous diary. The words from the diary, reproduced from an entry she made on October 29, 1943, are symbolized by the strong horizontals and verticals of the floor plan, which form a cagelike structure within which Anne seems trapped.

Anne's image was painted in black acrylic on a solid gray fabric, and the cagelike structure was created by appliquéd crisscrossing black ribbon. The red floor plan was accomplished through a combination of appliquéd red ribbon and embroidery. The words from Anne Frank's diary were stenciled in white acrylic on black linen. The graphlike pattern in the background and along the border refers back to the pattern on the cover of Anne Frank's actual diary.

4. REMEMBRANCE
Introductory   62″ × 93″   1989

This wall hanging serves as both an introduction to the Holocaust Wall Hangings series and as a summation. It is a collage of images and words taken from many of the other wall hangings. The Holocaust is here rendered via a hodgepodge of visual symbols associated with death: corpses, dismembered heads and limbs, train tracks, boxcars and barbed wire. In this nightmarish scene, the individual—such as Anne Frank—is lost in a depersonalized world where black prevails.

Many of the techniques employed in the Holocaust Wall Hangings are utilized here: painting, block printing, stenciling, sewing, appliqué, embroidery, and beading. Repeated horizontal embroidered metallic silver lines extending over the work from edge to edge symbolize barbed wire and serve to unify the wall hanging. The dedicatory words are spelled out all around the border. The Holocaust Wall Hangings are here explicitly dedicated to the memory of the artist's husband, Robert Liberman, who, as a member of the United States liberating forces, saw Dachau in 1945 and never forgot. The artist began working on the subject of the Holocaust following her husband's death in 1986.

5. TWO THOUSAND YEARS
Maps of the Holocaust   65" × 81"   1988

This map of Europe focuses on the destruction of two thousand years of Jewish life in Europe during World War II. The dates indicate when the Jewish communities destroyed in the Holocaust in various countries were established. The image of the lion is used as a symbol for the Jewish people. The red lion, the Lion of Judah full of life, shows that each community was established. The lion is gray and upside down to indicate that the community was destroyed.

The repeated image of the lion in the body of the work was block printed directly on the background fabric, but along the edges it was printed on swatches of fabric and then appliquéd. The borders of the European countries were embroidered in gray cotton floss. The red beads scattered over the surface symbolize the bloodshed.

6. KRISTALLNACHT
Maps of the Holocaust   69" × 80"   1989

The focus in this work is the night of November 9, 1938, when the Nazis launched a campaign of terror against the Jews of Greater Germany, setting fire to synagogues, destroying Jewish homes and businesses and killing Jews. The term *Kristallnacht* ("Night of Glass") refers to the broken glass of Jewish synagogues, homes and businesses resulting from this violence. The map depicts the area of Greater Germany. All the towns shown in the map were the sites of anti-Jewish violence.

Broken glass is symbolized in this work by a variety of means: first, by the block-printed images of shattered glass on the background fabric; second, by the shiny silver fabric defining the area of violence; and, finally, by the hundreds of irregularly shaped crystal beads which cover the area like shards.

7. THE EINSATZGRUPPEN
Maps of the Holocaust   86″ × 96″   1990

This map depicts the section of Nazi-occupied Europe where the *Einsatzgruppen*—a Nazi task force of mobile killing units—operated in 1941–1942. The four units which made up this task force, totaling three thousand men, followed the German army in its drive East. Their assignment was to round up and kill all the Jews along their routes. With systematic savagery, the *Einsatzgruppen* murdered hundreds of thousands of Jews.

The area where the *Einsatzgruppen* operated is rendered in red fabric; the shape and color of the area are reminiscent of a puddle of blood. The *Einsatzgruppen* are represented by a repeated image of a soldier pointing a gun, block printed in black acrylic on patches of fabric and appliquéd onto the red fabric. The names of some of the towns where the *Einsatzgruppen* operated were stenciled on. The area is strewn with block-printed bodies and shiny red beads symbolizing the carnage. The patterned background fabric of the wall hanging, with its white crosslike shapes on a black ground, connotes grave markers.

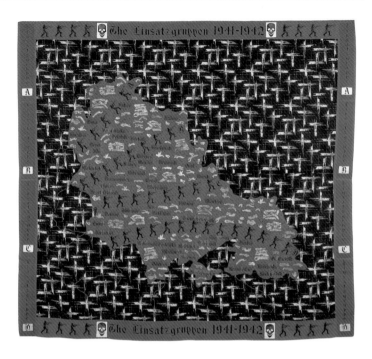

8. WANNSEE PLANS
Maps of the Holocaust   64″ × 84″   1988

This map of Europe shows the plans made by the Nazi officials gathered at Wannsee, a suburb of Berlin, in January 1942, to discuss the Final Solution to the so-called "Jewish Problem." The "Jewish Problem" was the very existence of Jews, regarded by the Nazis as a threat to Aryan racial purity. The Final Solution was to kill every single Jew in Europe.

The stripes on the background fabric were block printed in white acrylic with row upon row of human skulls. A map of Europe, embroidered in gray cotton floss interspersed with clear rochaille beads, is delineated over the area. The number noted by the Wannsee officials as representing the Jews in each area of Europe was stenciled on scraps of fabric which were appliquéd in the corresponding areas on the map. The total number of Jews marked by the Wannsee Conference for extermination—namely, 11,000,000—appears repeatedly along the black border.

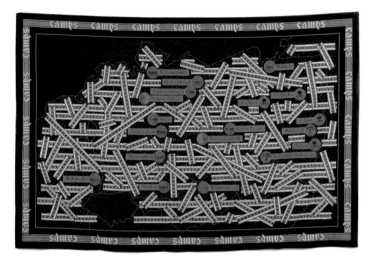

9. CAMPS
Maps of the Holocaust 65" × 99" 1991

Of the many hundreds of internment camps set up by the Nazis, a total of nineteen of the major ones are represented in this wall hanging, which indicates the different functions that these camps served. Of the nineteen camps, four (Belzec, Chelmno, Sobibor and Treblinka) were strictly killing centers and two (Auschwitz and Majdanek) were combination labor/death camps. The function of each camp is conveyed by the symbol attached to its name. The skulls signify death. The train tracks which fill the background serve as a reminder of the systematic way the Jews were transported to the camps.

The images attached to the names of the camps were created by means of block printing in acrylic on round patches of red fabric. The tracks were painted on rectangular patches of patterned gray fabric. The patches were appliquéd on the black background fabric. In addition to block printing, painting, and appliqué, this wall hanging also incorporates stenciling (in the names of the camps and in the repeated title "Camps"), embroidery (creating the borders of the countries with red cotton floss), and beading (tiny shimmering red beads are strewn over the area of Europe).

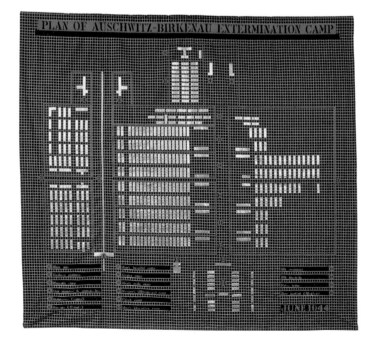

10. PLAN OF AUSCHWITZ-BIRKENAU
Maps of the Holocaust 97" × 109" 1991

The layout of the Auschwitz-Birkenau camp, one of six killing centers set up by the Nazis following the Wannsee Conference, is portrayed in this work. Auschwitz was designed not only as a killing center but also as a forced labor camp. The ramp, where new arrivals were separated for life, which meant forced labor, and for death, is represented here, as are the huts where those selected for forced labor were crammed. The gas chambers are also indicated.

This work was created by a combination of sewing, appliqué and stenciling. Each of the huts is separately represented by a rectangular patch of silver fabric. The gas chambers and crematoria are similarly indicated. The ramp is represented by an appliquéd silver ribbon, and the outline of the various parts of the camp was rendered by appliquéd red ribbon, symbolizing the fact that the electrified fences surrounding the camp were themselves instruments of death. The various areas of the camp are marked by numbers and described by stenciled labels at the bottom. The checks of the background fabric remind one of graph paper and serve to underscore the pedantic planning involved in the establishment and operation of Auschwitz, the largest and deadliest of the Nazis' death camps.

11. ROAD TO AUSCHWITZ
Maps of the Holocaust   85″ × 113″   1988

This map shows the many roads that led to Auschwitz, the deadliest of all the concentration camps. From north, south, east and west, vast numbers of human beings were transported to their death at Auschwitz. The boxcars covering the background symbolize the methodical way in which the Nazis pursued their goal of the Final Solution.

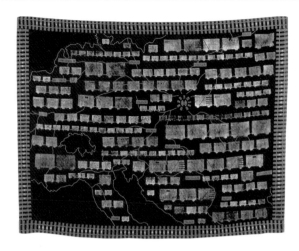

The repeated image of the boxcars, block printed in silver acrylic on patches of rough burlap and appliquéd onto the background, underscores the Nazis' relentless pursuit of their objective. The borders of Europe were embroidered in gray cotton floss, while the roads leading to Auschwitz from all directions are indicated by appliquéd red ribbon. Red ribbons also help form the image of the railroad tracks around the border. Auschwitz is marked by a glistening, faceted, red acrylic jewel, symbolizing blood and fire.

12. CROSS
Maps of the Holocaust   81″ × 81″   1996

The layout of the six Nazi death camps—Auschwitz, Belzec, Chelmno, Majdanek, Sobibor and Treblinka—is presented in this wall hanging in the form of a cross. The image of the cross begs the question: Where was God during the Holocaust?

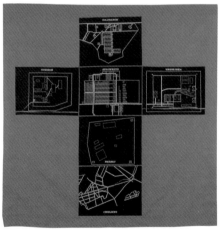

The camps are rendered through a combination of painting and embroidery. The names of the camps were stenciled in. The area of each of the camps is defined by a rectangular black piece of fabric appliquéd onto the red background. The stark color combination of red and black symbolizes bloodshed and death.

13. AUSCHWITZ EVACUATION
Maps of the Holocaust   64″ × 82″   1991

In view of the rapid advance of Soviet forces, the Nazis undertook the evacuation of Auschwitz in January 1945. This map pinpoints approximately two dozen of the camps to which Auschwitz inmates were evacuated by train. The open wagons around the periphery signify the fact that many were forced to travel in open railway wagons, exposed to the fury of winter, and hundreds died of exposure.

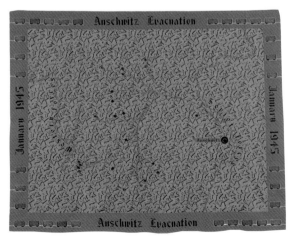

The background fabric of this wall hanging is gray, patterned with black lines whose movement connotes furious activity and confusion. The advancing Allied armies are represented by a line of appliquéd red triangles, while the evacuation routes leading to camps away from Auschwitz are rendered by appliquéd red ribbon. Auschwitz itself is punctuated by a large, faceted, red acrylic jewel, while tiny shimmering red glass beads are strewn over the whole area, symbolizing bloodshed. The open wagons were printed by means of linoleum blocks in black acrylic on gray fabric, then appliquéd. The words were stenciled with black acrylic.

14. SIX MILLION
Maps of the Holocaust   72" × 81"   1988

The number of Jews murdered by the Nazis in each part of Europe during the Holocaust is here represented by a number on one of the large dismembered arms scattered over the area. The dismembered arms symbolize death. The number of Jews killed in each area is represented as a tattoo. The allusion is to the tattooed ID numbers which the Nazis marked on the arms of their victims. The total of six million is indicated by the arms around the border.

The arms were block printed in varying shades of red acrylic on pieces of black fabric, which were appliquéd onto the background. The borders of the European countries are embroidered in red cotton floss. The beads scattered over the work help express the carnage. They are long and tubular, with an irregular surface, and are reminiscent of trees that have been chopped down, a symbol for death.

15. FATE OF THE GYPSIES
Maps of the Holocaust   62" × 80"   1990

Jews were not the only targets of the Nazi policy of ethnic cleansing. Like the Jews, the Gypsies were also regarded by the Nazis as belonging to an inferior race and thus endangering by their very existence the racial purity of the Germans. Hence the Gypsies, too, were targeted for annihilation.

This map utilizes the image of the hand—used by Gypsies to foretell the future—to convey the number of Gypsies murdered by the Nazis in various parts of Europe. The hands were block printed on black velvet to evoke the exoticism associated with Gypsies.

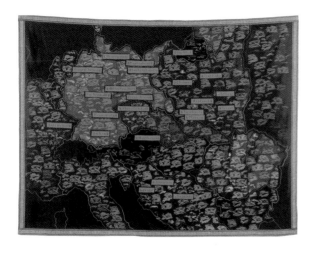

16. EUROPE 1945
Maps of the Holocaust   85" × 112"   1988

The continent of Europe is here portrayed as a graveyard at the end of World War II. The countries of Europe are strewn with bodies and some of the concentration camps where millions lost their lives are highlighted.

Each country of Europe is rendered in a different black fabric—cotton, linen, silk, velvet etc.—and appliquéd onto the background fabric. The borders between the countries were embroidered with variegated red cotton floss. Each of the concentration camps is punctuated by a glistening, faceted, red acrylic jewel, symbolizing blood and fire. The small red beads scattered over the map symbolize the carnage. The images of the bodies were done by means of linoleum blocks, which were carved and printed on the various pieces of black fabric. The same image of a body is printed again and again over the wall hanging to underscore that what happened in the Holocaust happened repeatedly across Europe.

17. SEARCH FOR SAFETY
Maps of the Holocaust   53″ × 110″   1989

This work focuses on the attempted escape of Jews from Nazi-dominated areas of Europe in the period 1933–1945, i.e., from the rise of Hitler to power in Germany through the end of World War II. The running figures, symbolizing escape, radiate from the Nazi center. The horizontal black stripes marking various areas of the world show the extent to which different countries restricted Jewish immigration (with the more widely spaced horizontals representing greater freedom of access). The number of Jews admitted by the various countries is indicated.

The running figures were block printed in gray acrylic on patches of black fabric, which were appliquéd on the black background fabric. The various countries which admitted Jews are represented by appliquéd red fabric. The borders outlining the continents were embroidered in variegated red cotton floss. Stenciling was used to render the words and numbers.

18. VOYAGE OF THE ST. LOUIS
Maps of the Holocaust   53″ × 86″   1989

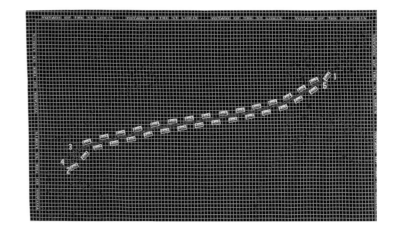

The reaction of many Jews to Nazi persecution was an attempt to escape, but as this work shows, there was no escape. The St. Louis was a German ship that left Germany in May 1939 with 936 refugees aboard, 930 of whom were Jews armed with certificates to enter Cuba. When the ship arrived in Cuba, however, only twenty-two of the Jewish refugees were admitted. The United States, where the refugees sought admission after being rejected by Cuba, refused admission to any of the refugees, so the boat turned around and returned to Europe. The refugees were discharged in Belgium. Most came under Nazi rule within twelve months and eventually perished in the Holocaust.

The voyage of the St. Louis from Europe to Cuba and back is represented by a repeated block printed image of the boat appliquéd along its route. The white-on-black graph squares of the background symbolize the glimmer of hope in a sea of despair.

19. REVOLT
Maps of the Holocaust   52″ × 64″   1989

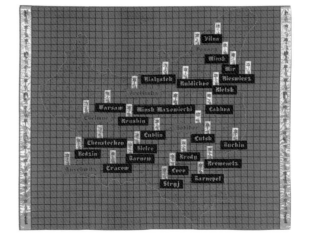

Although weakened and terrorized, some Jews rose in revolt against their tormentors. Both in the ghettos and in the camps, Jews joined together to strike back at the Nazis. The ghettos where Jews revolted are represented in this wall hanging by the black patches, while the camps where this occurred are represented by the red patches. An upraised hand holding the Star of David indicates revolt.

This work incorporates block printing, stenciling, sewing, appliqué, embroidery, and beading. The shimmering silver fabric on which the upraised Star of David is block printed symbolizes the glimmer of hope and contrasts sharply with the matte gray checkered background fabric. Shiny red glass beads are scattered over the area of the map, symbolizing bloodshed.

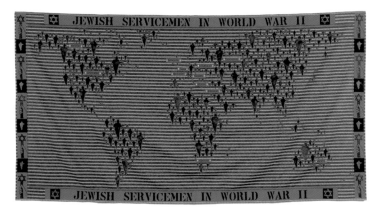

20. JEWISH SERVICEMEN IN WORLD WAR II
Maps of the Holocaust   57" × 110"   1991

Jewish resistance to the Nazis took place not only sporadically, as in the ghettos and camps, but also in the armed services of the Allies. This map shows how many Jews fought against the Nazis by participating in the various armed forces of the Allies. The repeated image of the soldier represents organized Jewish resistance to the Nazis.

The image of the soldier was block printed in black acrylic on red patches of fabric, which were appliquéd onto the background fabric. The repeated image of the soldier makes up the various continents, which are outlined by red cotton floss embroidery. The striped background fabric connotes the uniforms worn by camp inmates and symbolizes the Nazi power against which the Allies fought.

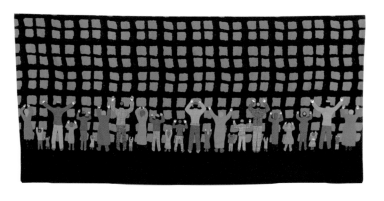

21. HANDS UP
Scenes of the Holocaust   46" × 97"   1989

In this scene, men, women, and children are standing facing away from the viewer with their arms upraised. They are facing a massive wall. Because their faces are invisible, the viewer's sense of the universality of their entrapment is heightened. Their stance, while indicating submission, also connotes supplication, and the wall they are facing, while implying "no escape," is reminiscent of the Wailing Wall. Perhaps at such a moment of despair, faith and prayer are the only way out.

The hands were painted on black scraps of fabric, then appliquéd. The figures were created by the appliquéing of fabrics of varying colors, patterns, and textures. The ground on which the group is standing is a solid black fabric, while the massive wall is rendered by means of a patterned fabric of irregularly shaped black horizontals and verticals on a gray ground. The overall tonality of the work is gray, symbolizing despair.

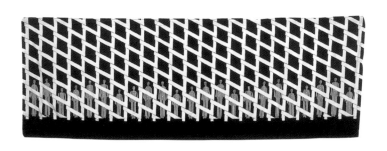

22. FENCED IN
Scenes of the Holocaust   48" × 137"   1989

The prisoners standing behind the massive fence pose an enigma: Are they different from one another or are they all the same? Their stiff poses and striped uniforms are the same. Even their faces appear the same. The only thing that seems to distinguish them from one another is their height. In each case, the height of the prisoner is just sufficient to allow him to stare out at the viewer through an opening in the fence. The depiction of the prisoners underscores the depersonalization that resulted from the Nazis' relentless pursuit of the Final Solution.

The massive fence is represented by a boldly patterned black and white fabric. The prisoners' uniforms were created by appliqué, with small buttons sewn on vertically along each top. The faces of the prisoners were created by the repeated printing on fabric scraps of a single linoleum block; the printed scraps of fabric were then appliquéd. The uniformity of the prisoners' faces symbolizes the dehumanization that took place in the Holocaust.

23. CART
Scenes of the Holocaust   47" × 56"   1989

Against the dark landscape of the Holocaust, a small child pulls a large cart upon which lies a corpse wrapped in white. Who is this child? And who is the dead person on the cart? Is it possibly the child's mother? And where are they? In the ghetto? And where are they heading? Most likely we will never know the answer to any of these questions because this child, like one and a half million other children, probably perished in the Holocaust.

This scene was created mostly by appliqué. The child's hand and face were block printed on black scraps of fabric, which were then appliquéd. At the intersection of the spokes of the wheel is a dull silver metal button, reminiscent of a rifle shell. The vastness of the patterned gray background fabric, contrasted with the smallness of the child, serves to underscore the helplessness of the individual in the Holocaust.

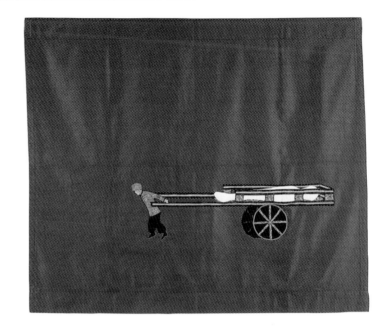

24. BOXCAR
Scenes of the Holocaust   75" × 88"   1991

The boxcar depicted here symbolizes the vast network of trains which the Nazis used to transport people during World War II. The image is that of a massive cattle car, all boarded up except for one small window through which the face of a girl is barely visible. The image in the window seems to be that of Anne Frank, possibly on her way from Holland to Auschwitz or from Auschwitz to Bergen Belsen, where she perished. The boxcar and Anne Frank's image in it concretize the destiny of the millions whom the Nazis shipped in boxcars to their deaths. The contrast between the massive boxcar and the fragile image in the window conveys the isolation and dehumanization of the individual in the Holocaust.

The boxcar and tracks were created by appliquéd fabric. A gray moiré fabric makes up the body of the train, its panels delineated by appliquéd silver ribbon. Striped gray taffeta was used for the tracks. Metallic silver buttons punctuate the panel housing the window like screws, indicating that it is sealed. Anne Frank's image was block printed on a separate piece of fabric and appliquéd, then covered by a layer of tulle to somewhat obscure the image in the window.

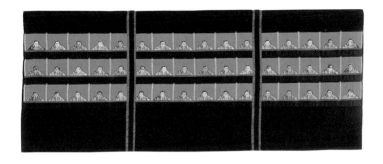

25. BUNKS
Scenes of the Holocaust   23″ × 56″   1989

Depicted against a massive structure of vertical poles and horizontal bunks are human beings so depersonalized that they seem to have lost all semblance of individuality. Clad in their uniformly striped camp garb, they lie crammed together in identical poses on level upon level of identical bunks, and stare at us with a gaze that is uniformly uncomprehending.

The scene was created by a combination of block printing and appliqué. The gray rectangular area against which the bunks and inmates are silhouetted was appliquéd onto the black background fabric, and the vertical poles as well as horizontal bunks were created by appliquéd ribbon. The prisoners were block printed in white acrylic on black pieces of fabric, which were appliquéd. Only a single block of linoleum was carved and was repeatedly used to print the figures. This repetition symbolizes the dehumanization that took place in the Holocaust.

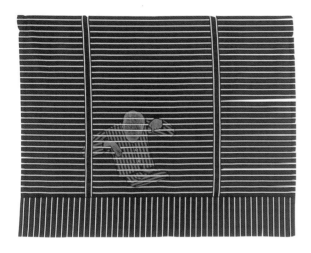

26. WIRE FENCE
Scenes of the Holocaust   45″ × 58″   1989

The wire fence used by the Nazis to imprison millions was often electrified. A mere touch of the fence would send a fatal electric charge through anyone who came in contact with it. While to many this represented an obstacle to freedom, others purposely touched the fence to escape what they considered a fate worse than death. We shall never know what kind of freedom the man depicted here sought, but by touching the fence, he succeeded in escaping a life he did not wish to continue.

The prisoner's figure was done by the appliquéing of pieces of striped gray fabric; his head and hands were block printed in gray on black burlap, then appliquéd. The starkness of the white-striped black fabric forming the foreground and fence stands in marked contrast to the muted appearance of the prisoner and suggests the underlying struggle between life and death.

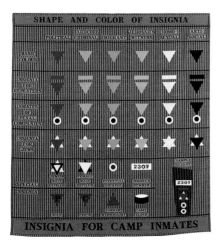

27. INSIGNIA
Scenes of the Holocaust   61″ × 56″   1994

The shapes and colors of insignia designed to be worn by inmates of Nazi concentration camps is here presented in the form of a grid. Across the top, the columns read: Political (red); Hardcore Criminal (green); Emigrant (blue); Jehovah's Witness (purple); Homosexual (pink); Antisocial (black). On the left margin, starting from the top, the categories are: Basic Colors, Insignia for Repeaters, Inmates of Penal Colonies, Insignia for Jews and Special Insignia. Some of the special insignia are illustrated and a sample sleeve with insignia appears at the lower right. The original document on which this presentation is based is in the camp museum at Dachau.

This wall hanging was created mainly by appliqué, the shapes of the various insignia rendered in appropriately colored fabric. The words were stenciled in black acrylic and the grid was created by painting. The background gray striped fabric evokes an image of the uniforms worn by camp inmates under the Nazis.

28. RACE DEFILER
Scenes of the Holocaust   44″ × 21″   1998

Two of the insignia worn by Jewish inmates of Nazi concentration camps are featured in this work. Both insignia represented "race defilers," a term used by the Nazis to describe Jews—male or female—suspected of having engaged in sexual relations with "Aryans." Both insignia combine a yellow triangle, which indicates "Jew," with a black triangle. The two insignia are based on illustrations found in a row of "Special Insignia" in the table of insignia of camp inmates contained in an original document at the camp museum in Dachau.

As in *TRIANGLES*, this wall hanging was created mainly by appliqué. The words "male," "female," "race defiler" and "Jew" were stenciled in silver acrylic. The background for the insignia is a striped fabric, which evokes the image of camp uniforms.

29. TRIANGLES
Scenes of the Holocaust   33″ × 114″   1998

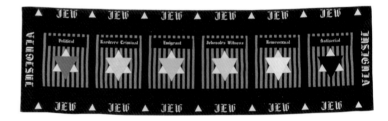

The focus here is on six of the insignia worn by Jewish inmates of Nazi concentration camps. The insignia were composed of triangular fabric patches of various designated colors—red for "Political," green for "Hardcore Criminal," blue for "Emigrant," purple for "Jehovah's Witness," pink for "Homosexual" and black for "Antisocial"—superimposed upside down upon the "basic" yellow triangle indicating "Jew." The presentation is based on the row entitled "Insignia for Jews" in the table of insignia of concentration camp inmates as seen in an original document in the camp museum at Dachau.

This wall hanging was created mainly by appliqué. The lettering was stenciled in silver acrylic. The triangles are mounted on striped fabric to suggest that the insignia were worn on camp inmates' uniforms. The words "Insignia" and "Jew," together with appliquéd yellow triangles, appear in the border.

30. YELLOW STAR
Scenes of the Holocaust   51″ × 51″   1994

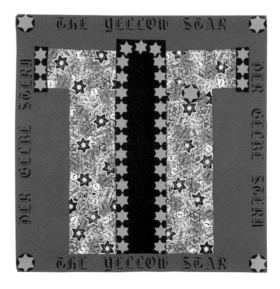

During the Nazi occupation of Europe, Jews were compelled to wear a badge to distinguish them from non-Jews. The required badge, which varied from region to region, was usually a yellow star on a black ground or a black star on a yellow ground, often with the reference to "Jew" in the local language indicated at the center of the star. This wall hanging treats the badge not as a badge of shame but rather as one to be worn with pride. The image here is that of a regal coat adorned with stars.

The shape of the coat was rendered by appliquéing a piece of black fabric onto the red background. Most of the stars in this work were created by means of block printing. Linoleum blocks were carved with the various designs and printed in black acrylic on patches of variegated yellow, which were then appliquéd in a lively collage. The yellow stars edging the front and sleeves of the coat were appliquéd to suggest a garland of flowers, or lei, a symbol of hospitality and farewell.

31. BOARDING
Scenes of the Holocaust　　46″ × 58″　　1994

Images—both photographic and art—of people boarding trains vie with one another for attention in this collage. The repetition of the images is designed to underscore the fact that what happened in the Holocaust happened repeatedly.

Both the photographic and the art images used in this work were transfer printed onto rectangular patches of solid gray cotton fabric, which were then appliquéd onto a background fabric. The image of a large group of faceless people boarding a train, which appears again and again in this work in various sizes, is taken from the artist's painting BOARDING (acrylic on stretched canvas, 30″ × 40″, 1987), which is part of her Holocaust Paintings series. The gray tonality of the work has a newsreel-like quality and symbolizes hopelessness.

32. SHOWERS
Scenes of the Holocaust　　46″ × 58″　　1994

"Showers" was the euphemism used by the Nazis to lure unsuspecting victims into the gas chambers. Photographic as well as art images related to the gassing and cremation of human beings form a patchwork of images claiming attention in this wall hanging. The repetition of images underscores the universality of the deceptiveness and brutality employed by the Nazis.

The images, whether photographic or derived from art, were transfer printed onto rectangular pieces of gray cotton, then appliquéd to the background fabric. The image of the line of women and children on their way to the "showers" above a heap of bodies derives from the artist's painting SHOWERS (acrylic on stretched canvas, 30″ × 40″, 1987), which is part of the artist's Holocaust Paintings series. The gray tonality of the work, as in its companion piece BOARDING, has a newsreel-like quality and symbolizes hopelessness.

33. GIFTGAS
Scenes of the Holocaust　　42″ × 48″　　1994

Giftgas is the German term for poison gas. Pictured in this wall hanging is a can of Zyklon B gas pellets, of the kind used by the Nazis at camps such as Auschwitz to gas millions of human beings. The term *Giftgas* is clearly visible on the can. The pellets were thrown by Nazi functionaries through an opening in the ceiling of the gas chamber and would turn into poison gas upon contact with the air, suffocating those trapped in the sealed chamber below. This method of mass murder was especially devised by the Nazis in pursuit of their goal of the Final Solution, namely, the annihilation of the Jewish people.

The photographic image of a Zyklon B can was transfer printed on fabric and appliquéd onto a patterned background fabric. The black and gray patterned background fabric was especially selected because its pattern suggests showerheads. The gas chambers were euphemistically called "showers" by the Nazis so as to more easily lead their unsuspecting victims to the slaughter. The term *Giftgas* was stenciled around the image of the Zyklon B can.

34. THE FINAL SOLUTION
Scenes of the Holocaust   **67″ × 67″   1990**

The progression of anti-Jewish measures taken by the Nazis in pursuit of the Final Solution is represented in this wall hanging as a four-step process. From evacuation and relocation in the upper left quadrant of the work, the scenes move clockwise to incarceration in camps, individual and group murder and, finally, to mass extermination by gas and crematoria. The four-step process is represented by scenes arranged in four rectangular panels, two horizontal and two vertical, against a black background. Because of the arrangement of the gray panels, the black background forms a swastika. The red border of the wall hanging bears the words "The Final Solution" as well as images of skulls.

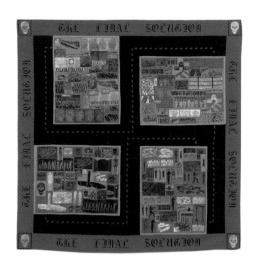

The various scenes were created by means of block printing. Dozens of linoleum blocks were carved with different images of persecution and printed with white or black acrylic on gray patches of fabric, which were assembled into rectangular panels. The thick red floss used to assemble the patches serves to divide the different scenes from one another and provides emphasis to each. A stenciled hand on the black background indicates the direction of the progression of anti-Jewish measures. The red border connotes blood and makes explicit the meaning of this wall hanging.

35. FIRE
Scenes of the Holocaust   **38″ × 47″   1990**

The image of an arm protruding from a crematorium underscores the crematorium's human connection. The arm here, like the arms of millions in the Holocaust, bears a tattoo. The tattoo reads "6000000" and thus reminds us that six million Jews perished in the Holocaust.

The crematorium, formed in black fabric appliquéd onto the red background, has a fiery red interior rendered in shimmering red silk. Tiny red glass beads sewn near the edge of the crematorium's open doors seem to reflect the fiery interior. The arm was block printed on a separate piece of fabric, which was then appliquéd. The number "6000000" was stenciled on. The image of the bricks was created by the use of a black-striped red fabric overpainted in acrylic with black vertical lines.

36. MONUMENTS
Scenes of the Holocaust   **55″ × 172″   1990**

The three crematoria facing us with their open doors invite us to probe the secrets they hold within. What unspeakable events took place here? These large black crematoria are gravestones marking the road of history, monuments which serve to remind us of humanity's dark past.

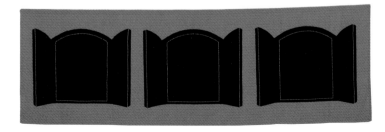

The images of the crematoria were created by appliquéd black fabric. Red stitching along the edge of the crematoria doors and the tiny glistening red glass beads edging the crematoria interiors suggest the glow of fire. The black-striped red fabric of the background represents the brick wall in which crematoria were housed in the camps. The red color of the background symbolizes blood and fire; the blackness of the crematoria symbolizes death.

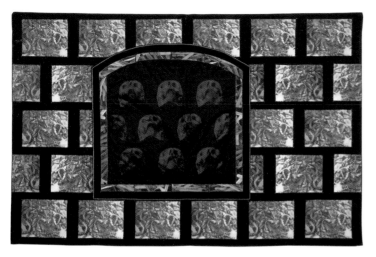

37. MEMORABILIA

Scenes of the Holocaust   48" × 74"   1995

Images of the dentures collected by the Nazis from the mouths of their victims and intended for reuse make up the wall in which a crematorium is set. The crematorium itself is edged with images of toothbrushes. Visible in the interior of the crematorium are human skulls, their teeth sharply defined.

The photographic images of dentures and toothbrushes were transfer printed on pieces of fabric, which were then appliquéd onto the black background fabric. The skulls were transfer printed from copies of the artist's drawing of a skull onto patches of fabric, then appliquéd. A semitransparent layer of a black gauzy fabric covers the interior of the crematorium, forcing the viewer to look closer at the cache of human skulls. The contrast between the clarity of the man-made objects—the dentures and toothbrushes—and the obscurity of the skulls serves as a reminder that man-made objects were more highly valued by the Nazis than human life and therefore had a better chance of surviving the Holocaust.

38. BELONGINGS

Scenes of the Holocaust   25" × 130"   1995

A collage of images associated with human hair makes up this panoramic wall hanging. Photographic images of implements usually associated with hair—combs, brushes, razors, scissors—are presented together with those of human hair, whether shorn, packed in bags or woven into mats. The depicted implements and the hair survived the Holocaust. The featured photograph of the twosome—the dark haired lady and the blond girl—reinforces the underlying element of "hair."

The photographic images were transfer printed on rectangular patches of fabric and then appliquéd onto the background fabric. The images are repeated, though in a variety of sizes, to underscore the universality of the destructiveness wrought by the Nazis. The featured photograph of the lady and girl was taken in Israel (then Palestine) in 1942, i.e., during the Holocaust. The girl was the artist, Judith, and the lady was her nanny, Batya. Batya had escaped from Poland and arrived in Israel (then Palestine) shortly before the outbreak of World War II. She immediately found employment as a nanny with Judith's family. Batya had left her elderly parents and young brother in Poland. Her parents were later murdered by the Nazis. Batya was Judith's personal link to the Holocaust. The emotional connection between Judith and Batya is clearly evident.

39. GOOD AND EVIL

Epilogue   45″ × 50″   1998

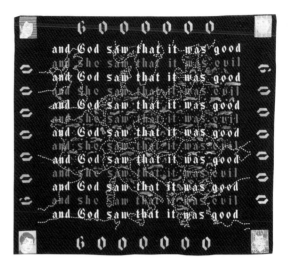

The starting point for this wall hanging was the biblical statement in Genesis that when He created the world, God "saw that it was good." By contrast, the artist probing the Holocaust cannot help but see the prevalence of evil. The biblical statement appears seven times in this work, once for each of the seven days of creation. That phrase is interspersed with "and she saw that it was evil," which reflects the artist's view. These two contrasting visions of the world are set in this wall hanging against the background of a map of Europe during the Holocaust. Bodies are strewn all over the area and a multitude of glistening red beads symbolize the carnage. The number "6000000"—a reference to the number of Jews who perished in the Holocaust—appears around the border, as do four of the artist's Self-Portraits of a Holocaust Artist.

This work combines stenciling, block printing, transfer printing, appliqué, embroidery, and beading. It raises a fundamental question: How can the biblical view be reconciled with the Holocaust?

40. POWER

Epilogue   21″ × 51″   1999

This work relates to Psalm 145:11: "*Of your power they will tell . . .*" Depicted are piles of artificial limbs, heaps of dentures and mounds of eyeglasses, all taken by the Nazis from their victims in the Holocaust. POWER raises the question: Why did God not use His power to help the weak?

The images were transfer printed from copies of Holocaust photographs onto patches of cotton fabric, then appliquéd. The wording was stenciled with silver acrylic paint.

41. PRAISE

Epilogue   21″ × 51″   1999

This work relates to Psalm 145:4: "*Each generation will praise your deeds . . .*" The imagery is from *Kristallnacht* ("Night of Glass") and Auschwitz. Depicted are destroyed synagogues, scorched Torahs and heaps of prayer shawls. PRAISE raises the question: While the Jews were devoutly praising Him, where was God?

The images were transfer printed from copies of Holocaust photographs onto patches of cotton fabric, then appliquéd. The wording was stenciled with silver acrylic paint. The appliquéd striped fabric and the knotted cording dangling down from the two bottom corners are designed to suggest a prayer shawl.

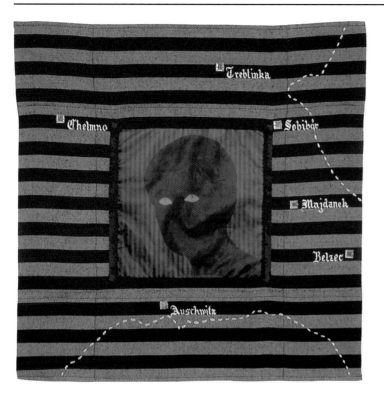

42. VANISHED

Epilogue   **21″ × 21″**   **1998**

This wall hanging incorporates a map on which are indicated the six Nazi death camps where millions died. A self-portrait of the artist appears at the center. In probing the Holocaust, the artist's personal identity is obscured because of her feeling of empathy with the victims. Only her eyes remain clear to see.

The artist's self-portrait was transfer printed onto white cotton from a copy of her *SELF-PORTRAIT OF A HOLOCAUST ARTIST #107* (acrylic on stretched canvas, 18″ × 18″, 1997). A semisheer black fabric helps obscure the artist's face. The borders of the map were embroidered with gray cotton floss and the names of the death camps were painted with white acrylic. Each of the death camps is punctuated by a clear square acrylic jewel. The background of the work is striped to evoke images of camp uniforms and wire fences from the Holocaust. The gray tonality of the work conveys a feeling of helplessness and despair.

43. HOLOCAUST ARTIST

Epilogue   **21″ × 113″**   **1997**

In this wall hanging the artist probes, through a series of eleven self-portraits, her own preoccupation with the subject of the Holocaust. The self-portraits portray the artist in various settings which evoke the Holocaust. From left to right she is seen peering through the window of a boxcar; staring from behind a barbed wire fence; looking into a map of Europe on which the six death camps are indicated; wearing a crown marked "Jew"; studying a map of Europe; looking through the eyes of Anne Frank; imprisoned behind bars; looking through a yellow Star of David; and, finally, in the last three self-portraits, personally vanishing as she immerses herself in the Holocaust.

The self-portraits incorporated in this wall hanging were transfer printed from eleven paintings belonging to the artist's series of Self-Portraits of a Holocaust Artist. The original self-portraits were done in acrylic on stretched canvas in 1997. The images as printed were appliquéd onto the black background fabric of the wall hanging. The words "Holocaust Artist," stenciled in silver acrylic, frame the work.

44. WITNESS

Epilogue   18″ × 26″   1998

The artist's eye is here superimposed upon that of Anne Frank in an expression of identification. Set against a map of Europe, the tracks leading Anne Frank on her journey to death pass over Anne's mouth, as if to silence her. But nothing, not even death, could silence the voice. Like her young subject, the artist, too, bears witness to the Holocaust.

This work was created through a combination of transfer printing, appliqué, embroidery, and beading. The portrait was transfer printed on white cotton from a copy of the artist's painting *SELF-PORTRAIT OF A HOLOCAUST ARTIST #102* (acrylic on stretched canvas, 18″ × 18″, 1997). The background of the wall hanging consists of a striped fabric which evokes images from the Holocaust: camp uniforms, wire fences and railroad tracks. The artist's identification with Anne Frank was heightened by the fact that the two were born the same year.

45. ID

Epilogue   21″ × 26″   1998

In this work, a self-portrait of the artist appears on an identification card similar to those which Jews had to bear under the Nazis. The large red "J" on the left half of the document (standing for "Jude," or "Jew") and the added middle name "Sara" on the right identify the bearer of the document as a female Jew. Jewish males' ID cards also bore the letter "J" but had "Israel" added as a middle name.

The ID card was transfer printed onto white cotton fabric from a reproduction of the artist's *SELF-PORTRAIT OF A HOLOCAUST ARTIST #100* (mixed media on stretched canvas, 20″ × 30″, 1997). The transfer printed image was appliquéd onto a red background fabric, on which are also appliquéd block-printed yellow Stars of David marked "Jude." The word "Jew" was stenciled in black acrylic around the border. Large glistening red beads, symbolizing bloodshed, are scattered over the red background.

How I Create Them
The Holocaust Wall Hangings

by

Judith Weinshall Liberman

AN OVERVIEW

The Holocaust Wall Hangings are works on fabric. In their conception, they fall mainly into two distinct groups. First, there are the *Scenes of the Holocaust*. These works refer more or less to the visible world; in the continuum between realistic and abstract, they are closer to the former than to the latter. In most of the *Scenes*, people take center stage. They are seen as either utterly isolated (as in *Boxcar*, *Cart*, *Wire Fence*) or as part of a totally depersonalized mass (as in *Bunks*, *Fenced In*, *Hands Up*). In either situation, the individual is portrayed as stripped of his/her humanity by the Holocaust.

In the second group, the *Maps of the Holocaust*, the Holocaust is depicted in more abstract terms. Places and numbers, as well as other symbols of destruction, take the place of the individual in telling the story. Often in these works, as in the *Scenes*, people appear (like the soldier in *Einsatzgruppen*, bodies in *Europe 1945*), but this is done within the broader context of place and time.

Like paintings, the Holocaust Wall Hangings are artworks designed to hang on a wall. Unlike most paintings which are done on canvas, the Holocaust Wall Hangings are loose-hanging rather than stretched on stretchers. There is a sleeve along the top of each wall hanging, through which a rod is inserted; when the wall hanging is displayed, the rod, which is longer than the wall hanging and protrudes on either end, rests on long nails hammered diagonally into the wall on each side. Although a more sophisticated method of hanging the Holocaust Wall Hangings—such as Velcro—would have been possible, I chose the rod method because of its simplicity and expressiveness. The idea of creating fabric works about the Holocaust was inspired in part by memories of the banners of the Third Reich flying over Nazi-occupied Europe. The idea of a banner hanging off a rod was therefore integral to the conception of the Holocaust Wall Hangings.

Stating that the Holocaust Wall Hangings are works on fabric may belie the wide variety of materials and techniques used in creating them. Among these techniques, some—such as painting and block printing, by means of which much of the imagery in the Wall Hangings was created—are normally associated with fine art. Stenciling is frequently utilized, as the Holocaust Wall Hangings are replete with lettering. Sewing, appliqué, embroidery and beading, which are traditionally associated with the world of crafts, play an important role in creating and enhancing the power of the works. And, finally, the possibility of transferring photographic and other images onto fabric has broadened the scope of expression far beyond what was possible through more traditional methods of fine art and craft.

THE BACKGROUND FABRIC

Unlike a tapestry, where the imagery is created by means of weaving threads of different colors and textures, a wall hanging is created on a base of ready-made fabric, which is normally uniform in coloration and texture. This fabric will here be called "the background fabric." The background fabric is store-bought and can be found in either the clothing fabric or in the decorating fabric section of a typical fabric store.

An important consideration in choosing the background fabric for a wall hanging, aside from the usual considerations of durability, stability, color-fastness, crease-resistance, responsiveness to steaming etc., is that the fabric be substantial enough to hold the variety of

materials which will be applied to it in the process of creating the work, such as appliqué, beading and embroidery. I often use heavy-weight cotton, such as black denim. Other favorite fabrics are sturdy cotton-polyester blends or even hefty woven polyester. I shy away from knits as background fabrics because they stretch.

If the imagery planned to be created by means of either painting or block printing will be created directly on the background fabric—rather than on other pieces of fabric which will then be appliquéd onto the background fabric—it is important to make sure that the background fabric will be absorbent and not be "stain repellent"; a fabric that has been treated for stain repellence will likely shed the paint used for the imagery sooner or later. The same holds true if stenciling or calligraphy is to be applied directly to the background fabric. In either case, if the imagery or lettering is planned to be created directly on the background fabric, testing a small swatch of the fabric to ensure that it is compatible with the application of paint will save many hours of labor and heartache.

Although most of the Holocaust Wall Hangings were created on solid-colored background fabrics (normally solid black or solid red), in some of the works a patterned fabric is used. In such cases, the pattern is often geometric. For example, in WANNSEE PLANS a diagonally-striped fabric was used, in JEWISH SERVICEMEN IN WORLD WAR II a horizontally-striped fabric was utilized and in both PLAN OF AUSCHWITZ-BIRKENAU and VOYAGE OF THE ST. LOUIS a checked fabric was employed. More free-form patterns constitute the background of such works as HANDS UP and GIFTGAS. In each case, the pattern of the background fabric was selected for its power to help convey the message of the projected wall hanging.

Because patterned fabric of a specific design is normally not a staple commodity, when I find a patterned fabric that seems promising, I buy a large amount of it to ensure I have enough on hand when I need it. I must confess that sometimes I buy the fabric before I have a specific wall hanging in mind. Yet, somehow, the fabric eventually gets used up. Perhaps that is because the fabric itself can be the inspiration for a wall hanging. An artist must always be receptive to his/her materials.

CREATING THE FRAMEWORK

The framework of each of the Holocaust Wall Hangings is the background fabric shaped in a manner tailored to the specific work. After selecting the background fabric for a projected wall hanging, I have to make two important decisions: What will be the overall format of the wall hanging? And what will be its dimensions?

Although the shape of a wall hanging can be freeform or an "odd" geometric one such as a triangle, a circle, etc., the Holocaust Wall Hangings have so far all been rectangular or square in format. A rectangular or square format serves the purpose of the Holocaust Wall Hangings series, which is to create "windows" through which the observer can see the Holocaust in its various manifestations. Each individual wall hanging reveals a different aspect of the Holocaust. There are *Scenes*, with their emphasis on the dehumanization of the individual in the Holocaust; there are *Maps*, with their revelation of what happened at a specific place—whether the place is the whole world, or the continent of Europe, or a group of European countries, or a city or a camp or even a single building—under Nazi domination. In all these cases, the rectangular or square format provides an excellent framework through which to view the Holocaust.

Where the format is rectangular rather than square, the vast majority of the Holocaust Wall Hangings are horizontal.

This format, again, seems uniquely tailored to the idea of revealing a panorama of *Scenes* and *Maps* of the Holocaust.

As for the size of the Holocaust Wall Hangings, they are fairly large in scale compared to "normal" wall-hung works of art. The initial impetus for creating works on a large scale was the idea that to understand the Holocaust, the viewer must be immersed in its various manifestations. My desire was to exhibit the works in a vast space whose walls would be covered with the works, offering the viewer no place to rest his eyes, no escape—thus mirroring the Holocaust itself. Creating the works in fabric seemed particularly well suited for such a vision.

When it comes to a specific work, however, the dimensions are determined by considerations deriving specifically from a desire to convey the idea of the work. For example, in CART, which portrays a boy pulling a corpse-laden cart in the ghetto, the smallness and isolation of the boy could be well conveyed without creating a huge wall hanging; on the other hand, in PLAN OF AUSCHWITZ-BIRKENAU, where the central idea is the creation by the Nazis of a vast and detailed death machine where millions perished, the idea itself dictated the large scale of the work.

When cutting the fabric, it is important to square off the edges, so that the wall hanging will be of the desired rectangular or square shape. This is not always easy. Resorting to ripping the fabric so as to get a straight edge does not always yield the wished-for results, since the weaving itself may be off. Often, in the larger works, two lengths of fabric have to be seamed together to create the required length or width, and this compounds the problem. Patience is the name of the game here. Use whatever mechanical means you can harness. Measure and remeasure. And, above all, do not despair (or so I tell myself).

Many of the Holocaust Wall Hangings have fabric

"frames"; i.e., the borders are distinguishable from the body of the work by being made of a different fabric or bearing words or images which form a distinct edging. Where the "frame" will be an extension of the background fabric of the wall hanging, I allow—along each one of the four edges—an extra border-width of fabric plus an inch in addition to the width of the border itself for folding over and stitching. Where the "frame" will be created from a fabric different than the background fabric, the framing fabric itself must be a border width plus a couple of inches wider than the intended width of the "frame" to provide for folding over and two seam allowances.

I usually finish the two side edges first, using a sewing machine. Most of the sewing in the Holocaust Wall Hangings is done by hand, because that allows for greater control. However, sewing the edges is different, simply because they are at the edges of the work.

Although I mark and sometimes even lightly baste the top and bottom "frame" edges to fold them over, I do not stitch them down until the very end. Reason? I may wish to appliqué, embroider, or bead the "frame" as the work progresses, and if the folded edge were stitched down, I would risk creating an obstruction to the hanging rod. I leave the bottom edge "open," too, to ensure that if a rod has to be inserted to weigh down the fabric when the work is on exhibition, the path is clear.

THE LAYOUT

I have often been asked whether I sketch out the Holocaust Wall Hangings before creating them. I usually do a small thumbnail sketch for each wall hanging, sometimes a bunch of different thumbnail sketches for a given work, and scribble some notes (legible only by me) about the central idea, the imagery to be used to convey

that idea, etc. I use these sketches and notes as a way of clarifying to myself what I want to say in a given work and how I want to say it. But I never sketch out the work the way it will be.

The only exception is in the *Maps*, where the map outline itself is drawn to scale ahead of time. I consider it important to be accurate in rendering a map. The way I see it, a map conveys information about a specific place at a specific time. Within the context of the Holocaust Wall Hangings, a map can be of the whole world or of a continent or of specific countries or of a city or of a camp or even of a building (as is the layout of the Annex in ANNE FRANK'S HIDING PLACE). In the case of the continents and various countries, I use a standard atlas and enlarge the desired map many-fold using techniques traditionally used by artists for enlarging. Similar techniques are used in maps of cities, camps or buildings. The enlarged map is usually rendered in pencil on strong paper (often in sections taped together) which is laid on top of the background fabric on the floor. I pin the map sketch to the fabric to prevent shifting. To do the tracing, I use a dressmaker's tracing paper—usually white, as the fabrics are dark—and bear down on the outline with either a ball-point pen or a tracing wheel. When I remove the sketch, the white outline of the map is visible on the fabric. My next step is usually to embroider the map, using cotton embroidery floss of suitable color in a modified chain stitch.

From here on, the process of creating the *Maps* is similar to that of creating any of the other wall hangings. It is a process of discovery. I spread the wall hanging on the floor in front of me. I interact with it. I create some images—usually on separate pieces of fabric to be appliquéd—place them here and there on the fabric and see the effect. Do the images express what I want to say?

Are the colors right, or should I change the hue, the saturation, the value? Should I add larger or smaller images? And where shall I place them and in what direction? How close together or far apart should they be? And does their texture support the image? Is it too similar to that of the background fabric?

These and many other questions run through my mind in the process of creating a wall hanging. Since the Holocaust Wall Hangings are large, I try to hold them together artistically through the harmony of repeated images which convey the underlying idea of the work; side by side with this harmony, and to avoid monotony, I try to create a variety of scale, of color, of texture, of direction, etc. I pay particular attention to movement through the imagery, allowing the eye to travel all over the work to grasp its meaning. There is no point in creating a vast work if the observer's eye will be stuck in one spot, is there?

In summary, the problems confronting me in creating the Holocaust Wall Hangings are no different from those I faced during the many years when my primary means of expression was painting: How do I create a work that expresses what I want to say and keeps the viewer's attention long enough to grasp it? This, I dare say, is the challenge confronting all artists, past, present, and future.

IMAGERY

The imagery for any given wall hanging is thought out generally in advance, during the sketching-and-scribbling stage. It is at this early stage that I try to decide upon imagery that will symbolize the underlying idea of the projected wall hanging. Often, especially in the *Maps*, I use a single image, repeated with variations throughout the work. The repetition underscores the fact that the atrocities that happened in the Holocaust happened over and over again.

Sometimes a single image imposes itself upon me right away. Thus, for ROAD TO AUSCHWITZ, the image that came immediately to mind was that of a boxcar. The people who were shipped to Auschwitz were crammed into boxcars for the long, arduous and often fatal journey; it therefore seemed fitting to have a boxcar convey the idea underlying the work. The image of the lion in TWO THOUSAND YEARS also seemed obvious: the proud Lion of Judah, a symbol of the Jewish People since biblical times, standing for the establishment of Jewish communities throughout Europe; the fallen lion conveying the destruction of these communities, some of them two thousand years old.

At other times, the image which would be the main bearer of the message in a particular wall hanging is harder to pin down. At such times, a variety of possible images—rather than the absence of any—presents itself to me. Making a choice requires me to imagine the work using this image or that. Such was the case in FATE OF THE GYPSIES, a wall hanging which, as its title suggests, deals with the fate of the Gypsies in the Holocaust. In preparation for this work, I had gone to the library and studied, in addition to facts and figures about Gypsies in the Holocaust, various books about the Gypsies generally, their origins, history, lifestyle, etc. In trying to come up with an appropriate symbolic image, the Gypsies' traditional nomadic existence captured my imagination, and I considered having a horse-and-carriage symbolize the Gypsies in the Holocaust. I also considered cards (as in Tarot), a storefront bearing the word "fortuneteller," a large family, a musical instrument . . . Suddenly, it hit me: a hand, a human hand with its palm facing the viewer. The hand would show the palm lines fortune-tellers study to predict a person's future. I wondered: Did the Gypsies predict their own fate in the

Holocaust? On each hand, I decided, would be revealed the number of Gypsy casualties in a particular part of Europe. The symbol of the hand would be a reminder that, hidden beneath the large numbers, were individual victims, men, women and children.

Once I decide upon the imagery, I have to determine what means I will use to create it. The choices are rich. First and foremost, since the Holocaust Wall Hangings are works on fabric, the possibility of creating the images themselves from "unadulterated" pieces of fabric immediately suggests itself. The images of the figures in such works as HANDS UP and FENCED IN were largely created by means of small pieces of fabric especially cut and appliquéd to suggest clothing. The images of the crematoria in MONUMENTS were created from large pieces of black fabric cut to shape and appliquéd onto the striped background fabric. Creating the images of triangles in INSIGNIA, TRIANGLES and RACE DEFILER was naturally accomplished by appliquéing triangularly-shaped pieces of fabric onto the background fabric.

Where pieces of fabric are used for appliqué, I usually back them with iron-on interfacing to make them more substantial and stable. An exception is a case such as the huts cut from formed fabric in PLAN OF AUSCHWITZ-BIRKENAU; the heat required to bond them to the iron-on interfacing would damage them. I like to edge each piece to be appliquéd with a satin stitch so as to avoid frayed edges and give the piece a finished look. These techniques of backing and edging fabrics are also used where the pieces are appliquéd after being painted on, printed, or used as a base for image transfer, as discussed below.

Lengths of ribbon are another way of using "unadulterated" fabric to create images in the Holocaust Wall Hangings. The layout of the city of Amsterdam in ANNE FRANK'S AMSTERDAM is entirely made of appliquéd

silver ribbon. Ribbon is also used to create much of the layout of the building and cage-like structure in ANNE FRANK'S HIDING PLACE. In works such as ROAD TO AUSCHWITZ, appliquéd ribbon is used in creating an image of railroad tracks around the border.

Another method of creating images for the Holocaust Wall Hangings is painting. The painting can be done directly on the background fabric or on a separate piece of fabric, which would then be appliquéd onto the background fabric. In each case, it is important to test the fabric to make sure the paint will adhere to it without flaking off. Natural fibers such as cotton, burlap, and linen are most compatible with paint. The hands in HANDS UP were painted on small pieces of fabric, which were then appliquéd onto the background fabric. Anne Frank's image in ANNE FRANK'C HIDING PLACE was also painted. The paints I use in the Holocaust Wall Hangings— whether for painting, block printing, or stenciling and calligraphy—are artists' acrylics. Artists' acrylics do not damage the fabric nor render it stiff, and have a track record for stability and durability.

Most often the images that appear in the Holocaust Wall Hangings are created by means of block printing rather than painting. Block printing has an obvious advantage over painting in the context of these works. Although carving a block for printing is labor-intensive, once the block is carved its image can be printed over and over again, both in the same wall hanging and in other works. The unpredictability of the exact appearance of a given print—which is due to various factors including humidity and pressure—makes it possible to achieve the variety I crave in the repeated imagery of many of the Holocaust Wall Hangings.

The blocks and sheets I use for block printing are made of linoleum rather than wood. Linoleum has several advantages over wood as a material for block printing in the Holocaust Wall Hangings. For one thing, linoleum is softer and easier to cut. It does not have a grain. It is less costly than wood. But its main advantage for me is that linoleum blocks can be purchased in a large variety of pre-cut sizes, and do not have to be especially sawed. I keep a drawer full of linoleum blocks and linoleum sheets of various sizes on hand so I can start creating images for a wall hanging at a moment's notice. For carving, I use an old set of Japanese carving tools that have surgical steel blades.

In preparing for block printing, it is crucial to remember to carve into the block a mirror image of the desired final image, because the process of printing naturally reverses the image as carved. This is especially important where the image includes letters or numbers. It is also advisable to preplan the color of the fabric on which the image will be printed and the color of the paint that will be used in printing, because that will determine what portions of the block should be carved out (so as to accept no paint) and what parts should not.

Image transfer is a relatively new and exciting method of creating fabric images for the Holocaust Wall Hangings. Image transfer makes it possible to transfer images directly from paper onto fabric. The first step in the process of image transfer is to copy the desired image in reverse (mirror image) onto paper using either a color copier or an ordinary copying machine. (An image printed on your office or home printer would probably not be suitable, as the printing ink will tend to bleed.) You cover the paper image with a layer of a creamy liquid called "transfer medium" and place the paper face down on a piece of prewashed light-colored cotton fabric, smoothing the paper and pressing gently all over to ensure adhesion. You wait twenty-four hours and then proceed to wet the back of the paper and rub it off in order to expose the image. You may have to rub the paper off repeatedly, as it stubbornly clings to the image and obscures it. Eventually a clear image will emerge on your fabric.

The image-transfer technique allows for the transfer onto fabric of images of varied etiology. What I particularly like about the technique in the context of the Holocaust Wall Hangings is that it allows for the use of photographic and art-based images. I have used strictly photographic images in BELONGINGS, and a combination of photographic and art-derived images in such works as BOARDING, SHOWERS, and MEMORABILIA. In the latter three works, the art images were derived from my own paintings and drawings. Image transfer thus allows me to integrate my own nonfabric artworks into the Holocaust Wall Hangings.

Image transfer is sometimes accomplished by means of copying an image onto a special paper, placing the paper face down on a prewashed piece of cotton fabric and ironing the back of the paper with a hot, dry iron. Although this technique of image transfer is much less time consuming, I prefer the clarity and finished look of the more arduous technique described above.

STENCILING

While I have not used stencils to create the imagery in the Holocaust Wall Hangings, stenciling has been used extensively in these works to render the letters, numbers, and some symbols (e.g., a pointing hand to indicate direction in THE FINAL SOLUTION). The title of a specific work—as in ANNE FRANK'S AMSTERDAM—is sometimes incorporated into the wall hanging, usually in the border of the work. In REMEMBRANCE, a dedication of the Holocaust Wall Hangings to my husband, Robert's, memory is spelled out all around the border, while the body of the work itself incorporates the title of the series, etc. The names of cities, ghettos and camps, the dates of the establishment of Jewish communities in various parts of Europe, the number of Jews planned for extermination by the Wannsee conference, the number of Jews and Gypsies who perished in the Holocaust, all appear in one wall hanging or another, and stenciling is the technique normally used for that purpose.

Letter stencils (which normally also include numbers) are readily available in a well-stocked art supply store. The stencils usually consist of heavyweight paper sheets, with perforations in the shape of letters and numbers . There is an array of letter styles (fonts) to choose from, as well as letter sizes. I usually get a package that has a variety of letter sizes of the desired letter style, so I will have them on hand when the need arises. For the Holocaust Wall Hangings I have used Old English style lettering, which looks Germanic, as well as Roman and sans serif lettering. Stencils may have to be replaced on occasion, as the edges of the letters tend to fill with paint after they have been used a few times. Heavy plastic stencil sheets, from which the paint could be scraped off, would be preferable, but are a rarity.

The most important thing to do once you have determined the style and size of lettering you want to use is to ensure proper spacing between letters (or numbers) and between words. This I do first on paper, using a sturdy tracing paper. I draw a long, straight horizontal line on a sheet of paper. The line will mark the bottom of most of the letters. Using the stencil and a sharp pencil, I proceed to trace the first letter, marking the desired spacing between it and the next letter by drawing a light vertical line where the next letter will begin. After I draw the next letter, with its left edge touching the vertical line, I study the spacing and determine whether I like it or not. Should the new letter be moved closer to the previous one or

farther away? The important considerations here are mostly aesthetic, although, of course, projecting the total length of the wording may require me to change the spacing or even the size of lettering to be stenciled. Similar considerations apply to spacing between words. The obvious advantage of using a pencil at this stage is that the lettering can be easily erased. I have not found the perforated holes in stencil sheets, designed to be a guide to proper spacing, particularly useful. Studying the actual spacing at each step is my chosen way.

Once the lettering has all been drawn on paper, it has to be traced onto the fabric. That fabric may be part of the background or "frame" fabric, or it may be an extraneous length of fabric to be appliquéd to the wall hanging at a later stage. In either case, it is important to start by taping or basting a long, straight line on the fabric, which will correspond to the long, straight horizontal line initially drawn on the paper to mark the bottom of the lettering. (Needless to say, the line on the fabric must take into account proper distance from the edge, adequate seam allowance etc.). Before pinning the paper to the fabric, I determine the center of the lettering and the center of the fabric, and mark each. I then match up the two centers and make sure that the long horizontal line on the paper matches up with the line on the fabric. After the paper is pinned in place, I use a dressmaker's white tracing paper and a ballpoint pen or sharp pencil to trace the letters. The tracing is more accurately done if the original stencil form is used, placed appropriately over each letter and allowing for the letter to be properly redrawn.

The next step is to apply paint to the letters within the traced outlines. For that purpose, a suitable paint color must be chosen. To make the wording more easily legible, I normally select a color that will contrast with the background, such as white or silver on a dark fabric, and black on a lighter-colored fabric. The paints used are artists' acrylics, applied with a special stiff stenciling brush. The paint has to be applied sparingly, with a stippling motion; too much paint will cause the paint to ooze out beyond the edges of the letter. Usually, applying the lighter colored paints, such as white or silver, to a dark fabric requires a second application of paint. To ensure that the lettering is completely dry before applying a new coat of paint, I first finish all the lettering and then go back and retrace my steps.

I have rarely had occasion to use calligraphy, i.e., free-hand lettering, in the Holocaust Wall Hangings. At times a particular shape, such as one used in punctuation, was not readily available. On such occasions, I drew the required shape on a piece of paper and traced it onto the fabric in a manner similar to that described above. Experimenting directly on the background fabric could be hazardous.

EXPRESSIVE / DECORATIVE ELEMENTS

Beading can be viewed as an important decorative element used in the Holocaust Wall Hangings. In many of the works, beads scattered throughout the work or concentrated in a specific area provide a sparkle which contrasts with the flat surrounding fabric and imagery and give the work added texture and dimensionality. Thus, the faceted acrylic jewel marking the camp in ROAD TO AUSCHWITZ and those punctuating the tracks in ANNE FRANK'S JOURNEY, as well as the round beads scattered throughout such works as TWO THOUSAND YEARS and even the elongated tubular beads which cover SIX MILLION, can be regarded as decorative.

While the beading in the Holocaust Wall Hangings is decorative, an important reason for my use of beads in various works has been their expressive power. The faceted red jewel marking Auschwitz in ROAD TO AUSCHWITZ symbolizes blood and fire; the same goes for the faceted jewels along the tracks in ANNE FRANK'S JOURNEY, leading Anne Frank toward her death. The round red beads scattered throughout many of the Wall Hangings, such as TWO THOUSAND YEARS and CAMPS and FATE OF THE GYPSIES, symbolize drops of blood. And the textured elongated tubular beads which cover SIX MILLION represent trees which have been chopped down, a symbol for death.

All the beads used in the Holocaust Wall Hangings are sewn rather than glued on. I do not trust glue to last as long as thread, and have therefore avoided its use in any way in these works. By definition, a bead has two holes. The thread, which emerges from the base fabric, goes in one hole of the bead and out the other, then reenters the base fabric and is knotted in the back. I usually sew each bead on separately to prevent a mishap to one bead from affecting any of the others. Every bead is sewn two or three times to ensure that it is firmly attached.

Embroidery is used in many of the *Maps*, usually in a modified chain stitch, to mark the borders between different countries. I use cotton embroidery floss, applied with an embroidery needle. Sometimes tiny beads are interspersed between the embroidery stitches to add sparkle and definition. While the embroidery has its decorative aspect, it serves an expressive purpose in the context of the Holocaust Wall Hangings.

The color used in the Holocaust Wall Hangings can also be regarded as decorative. The palette employed in these works is mostly black, gray, and red. The juxtaposition of a saturated red against black and gray is visually exciting. In a handful of works, such as YELLOW STAR, INSIGNIA, TRIANGLES, and RACE DEFILER, bright colors are used.

However, here again, the expressiveness of the color plays a vital role in my work. Yellows are used in *YELLOW STAR* because the work deals with the symbols which Jews were forced to wear under Nazi rule. In such works as *INSIGNIA*, *TRIANGLES*, and *RACE DEFILER*, bright colors are used to show the colors of insignia dictated by the Nazis for camp inmates. Finally, in the vast majority of the Wall Hangings, the limited palette of red, gray, and black expresses the Holocaust: Red symbolizes blood and fire; gray, suffering and despair; black, death.

EXHIBITING THE WORKS

During an exhibition of the Holocaust Wall Hangings, I noticed that a teenager who had come to the museum to view the show with his high school class was studying the works intently. I was pleased to see his great interest and asked if he had any questions. The young man hesitated a moment, then blurted out: "How come you don't sign them?"

I turned over the bottom right corner of one of the works to show my visitor that the works are "signed." He seemed relieved, even though the artist's name appeared only on the back. But then his curiosity took over again. Why, he wanted to know, don't I sign the works on the front, the way artists usually do with their work?

The young man's query made me realize that I had never even considered signing my name on the front of any of the Holocaust Wall Hangings. I had signed the front of my paintings for years, but, somehow, the Holocaust Wall Hangings seemed different. On further reflection I realized that once I had created a wall hanging, it felt to me like a sacred object. I could not explain to myself why that was so. (Was it because each one was a memorial to the death of millions?) Yet, although I could

not figure out *why* I had this feeling of awe, I was certain of one thing: Signing a Holocaust Wall Hanging on its face would feel sacrilegious. I simply could not do it.

So I "sign" each wall hanging on the back. For that purpose, I use a linoleum block which I carved (in mirror image) with my name, including my maiden name, "Judith Weinshall Liberman." I carved this block back in 1988, when I first started creating the Holocaust Wall Hangings. When I complete a wall hanging, I use the block to print my name near the corner of the bottom hem, using artists' white acrylic paint. To make sure the paint does not seep through to the front, I temporarily insert, before printing, a small piece of cardboard into the hem where the print is projected. Each year I carve (in mirror image) a new linoleum block with the year (1988, 1989, etc.) and print that either under or next to my name. And, voilà, the wall hanging is "signed."

Many visitors to exhibitions of the Holocaust Wall Hangings have commented on the size of the works and asked how I store them. The Holocaust Wall Hangings are, on average, so much larger than "normal" works of art that showing all of them simultaneously, even at a museum, has proven impossible so far. The most I have shown at the same time has been a group of thirty-seven works, and that was in a fairly large museum where both floors were dedicated to the works. But while exhibiting the Holocaust Wall Hangings requires a large amount of space—i.e., long, unbroken walls and tall ceilings— storing them does not. Because they are works on fabric, they can be easily folded and stacked one on top of the other in a fairly small space.

When preparing for an exhibition, I press each wall hanging carefully, then refold it and pack the works in suitcases, making sure that the heavier works are at the bottom. (Rolling them for shipment does not seem practical because of their size). When the works are hung at the exhibition, I sometimes have to steam out creases, which I do rather easily with a small handheld electric steamer.

When on exhibition, each wall hanging is suspended from a rod inserted through a sleeve at the top. The rod protrudes a few inches on either end and rests on long, strong nails hammered diagonally into the wall. Brackets through which the rod can be inserted are a costlier but neater method of hanging, and allow the works to hang away from the wall. The rods are made of wood and I ask each museum to prepare them from a list of lengths I provide and to paint them with an acrylic paint to match the walls. Unfinished wood could damage the works, and shipping rods back and forth is usually costlier than acquiring and preparing them. A good uniform diameter for the rods is 1 3/8 inches, which makes for a rod strong enough to hold even some of the heavier works without bowing. I sew plastic rings along the top at the back of each wall hanging—one at each end and one at the center—to carry the weight when needed. Even when the rings will not be required for suspension, they are useful in identifying the top of a folded wall hanging.

A wall label, whose text I prepare, accompanies each wall hanging while on exhibition. In addition to the information usually appearing on museum and gallery labels—i.e., the artist's name, the title, the medium and the year—the labels that accompany the Holocaust Wall Hangings also discuss the historical background and other aspects of the work. Art speaks for itself, but insight into the artist's way of thinking, coming straight out of the artist's mouth, seems to be deeply appreciated.